The Author

Hugh Popham was descended from a distinguished family of naval men – his most illustrious forebear established the Popham code that was used at the battle of Trafalgar. He wrote widely on naval matters after the War and was also a published poet and the editor of Erskine Childers' sailing logs. He died in 1996.

SEA FLIGHT

THE WARTIME MEMOIRS
OF A FLEET AIR ARM PILOT

HUGH POPHAM

New Introduction by David Hobbs

Seaforth
PUBLISHING

Copyright © Hugh Popham 1954
Introduction copyright © David Hobbs 2010
This edition first published in Great Britain in 2010 by
Seaforth Publishing,
Pen & Sword Books Ltd,
47 Church Street,
Barnsley S70 2AS

British Library Cataloguing in Publication Data
A catalogue record for this book is available from the British Library

ISBN 978 1 84832 055 0

First published by William Kimber and Co Ltd, London, in 1954

Printed and bound by the MPG Books Group, UK

CONTENTS

DEDICATION

To those who are not mentioned in the following pages,
and to those who are, I make whatever
apology is fitting. To all of
them I dedicate
this book

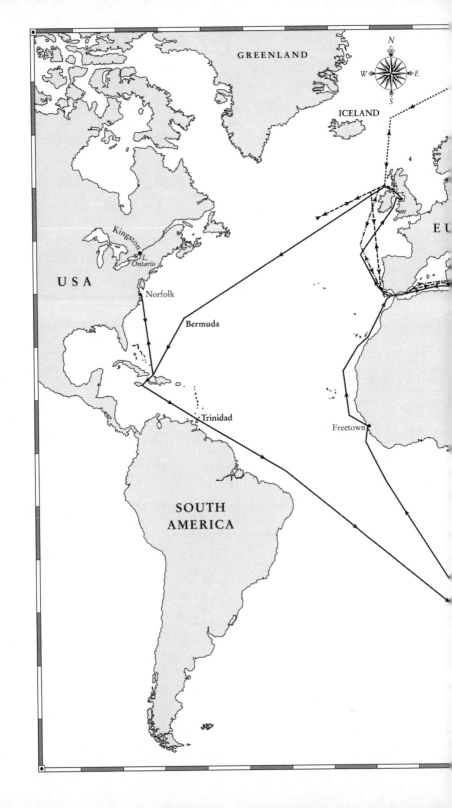

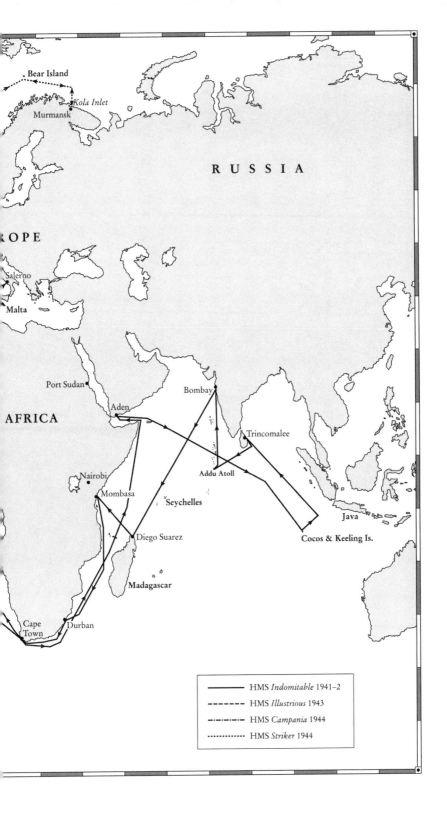

Bear Island

Kola Inlet
Murmansk

RUSSIA

ROPE

Salerno

Malta

Port Sudan

AFRICA
Aden

Bombay

Trincomalee

Nairobi

Addu Atoll

Mombasa

Seychelles

Java

Diego Suarez

Cocos & Keeling Is.

Madagascar

Cape Town
Durban

——————— HMS *Indomitable* 1941–2
- - - - - - - HMS *Illustrious* 1943
–·–·–·–·– HMS *Campania* 1944
·············· HMS *Striker* 1944

New Introduction

THIS wonderful memoir was the first account by a wartime naval pilot of his experiences flying fighters from the decks of aircraft carriers, and the author's remarkable powers of observation and gifted style of writing allowed him to describe his unique perspective with particular clarity and humour. Many have followed it but none have matched its ability to draw the reader into the events as they unfold. I can trace my own aspiration to become a pilot in the Royal Navy from the first time that I read this book.

Hugh Popham was studying law at Cambridge when he volunteered to become one of the early RNVR (Air) officers in 1939. He joined the Royal Navy's Fleet Air Arm at a time when it had only four hundred front-line pilots and it had only double that number when he joined his first squadron in September 1941. He was a member of the first pilots' course to be trained by the Empire Air Training Scheme in Canada and he was one of the first to be taught to fly Sea Hurricanes at the fighter pilots' school at RNAS Yeovilton. This was the Navy's most potent fighter in 1941 but there were only thirty-four of them in front-line service.

The Royal Navy had finally resumed full control of its carrier-borne aircraft in May 1939 after the failure of 'dual control', instigated in 1918. During that period, the RN had been responsible for operations at sea with the RAF overseeing administration, procurement and training ashore. Hugh's instructors at RNAS Yeovilton were the survivors of the pre-war generation who had fought the early campaigns in Norway and the Mediterranean and who had seen their colleagues shot down in aircraft that were both obsolescent and out-numbered, fighting a new form of naval warfare. At first, the RNVR officers were the new boys, trained in numbers that filled the gaps in the pre-war squadrons. Within four years the Fleet Air Arm expanded tenfold, by far the greater number of the 4,000 pilots in the front line squadrons being temporary officers from Britain, New Zealand, Canada, Australia and South Africa. Few of them had any previous naval experience and their training with the RAF and in Canada left little time for them to assimilate a wider knowledge of ships' routines and the way in which the Navy was organised. The need to learn new techniques was not confined to the young reservists, however, and senior officers appointed in command of aircraft carriers found themselves having to find new ways of understanding and leading the young men who had quickly become the experts in the new tactics of a very different form of naval warfare.

Popham's story is told with exceptional clarity as he describes his progress from initial training at HMS *St Vincent* in Gosport, through flying training to life in 880 Naval Air Squadron, a fighter unit embarked in a fleet carrier. His eye for detail and skill as a writer allows him to bring situations and events to life and draw the reader into the story as if he were there. His loyalties gradually expand from the friends on his course, his squadron and ultimately to his ships, especially HMS *Indomitable,* as he comes to terms with service life. It is a very human story in which he reveals both excitement and his innermost doubts, especially when friends and those around him are killed. His first book, an anthology of poems entitled *Against the Lightning* was written while he was serving in *Indomitable.*

Sea Flight is helped by its finite structure, beginning with basic naval training as ratings, followed by flying training where we feel the excitement he felt as each stage was successfully completed and share his trepidation before his first deck landing. Sea-time in four aircraft carriers makes up the middle of the story which ends when he was appointed to a 'desk' at the Admiralty.

He describes people with such shrewdness and insight that we feel we know them, especially 880 Squadron's commanding officer, the South African Lieutenant Commander F E C Judd, RN. Sometimes his most effective descriptions are understated, as when he refers to 880's only rating pilot as living a 'shadow existence' between the other pilots in the wardroom and the squadron's ratings, mostly aircraft mechanics who worked in the hangar. Even the broken back Popham suffered when he bailed out of a Seafire after a mid-air collision gives an insight into life in a wartime emergency hospital and finds him waddling ashore to the pub in a plaster-cast like a straight-jacket.

Although it is one man's story, the thread of the Fleet Air Arm's rapid expansion runs through *Sea Flight* and the reader can trace the development of naval aircraft from the obsolescent equipment of 1941 to more specialised and capable aircraft later in the War. RNVR pilots progress from being the 'junior boys' to experts in the new form of naval warfare, many of whom commanded squadrons by 1945, earned the respect of their longer-serving RN captains and commanders and joined the post-war regular Navy.

This book can be read as an exciting wartime 'yarn' with its fair share of action but there is another, deeper dimension and it stands as an eye-witness account of a period of rapid change in the Royal Navy; when battleships gave way to aircraft carriers and their air groups as the arbiters of sea-power. There is insight in the descriptions of operations and the progress of the War, especially during the aircraft ferry runs to the Dutch East Indies and Operation Pedestal, the biggest Malta convoy, in 1942.

Sea Flight reflects the author's pride in having served in the Fleet Air Arm of the Royal Navy, a Branch of the Service that faced danger even in the everyday operation of aircraft from ships. I have read my original copy many times before, during and after my own naval flying career and continue to find it as illuminating and absorbing as ever. I am delighted that Seaforth Publishing has decided to re-publish it for a new generation of readers to enjoy.

David Hobbs, MBE,
Commander Royal Navy (Retired)
Former Deputy Director and Curator of the
Fleet Air Arm Museum

The Making of a Pilot

PART ONE

The Making of a Pilot

I

FROM the roof-tops of H.M.S. *St. Vincent* in that high summer of 1940, we watched the bombs come tumbling down from 20,000 feet, and pointed a Lewis gun, somewhat optimistically, at the tiny silver toys that had let them go. We could see them all the way, turning over and over in the bank-holiday sunlight, growing larger and larger, and falling directly on to our upturned faces.

"Oh Jesus!" Jock said in a shocked voice; and Barry turned to the two of us, his hand outstretched.

"Well, goodbye, men," he said. We had not yet learnt to distrust Barry in a situation like this. We shook hands quickly, and cowered down behind the sandbags and waited.

We waited for several hours or days. Jock muttered: "They're taking a perishing long time to come doon." We glanced up, and saw the bombs quite suddenly go slanting off over the harbour. A second or two later they landed with a crumph on the town of Portsmouth, a good mile away.

We began, rather sheepishly, to talk of other things.

The next day the war came a step closer. The bombs started their long fall from farther away and landed on top of an ack-ack battery opposite the main gate of the barracks.

The daylight, and later the night, raids were only a part of the pattern which our lives had so dramatically, and recently, adopted. A month before I had been sitting Part I of the Law Tripos at Cambridge and trying to make some acceptable connection in my mind between Professor

Lauterpacht's "International Law" and the international anarchy which was in full swing on the other side of the channel. The examiners did not require me to make such an effort, and I was not really surprised to learn that I had only been awarded a Second. A month before Jock had been in a solicitor's office in Edinburgh, and Barry in a repertory company in the Midlands. Now, already, these past eccentricities had been rubbed down, disguised, by the sartorial absurdities of bell-bottomed trousers and jumpers and collars with the three blue lines that did (or did not) represent Nelson's three victories of Copenhagen, the Nile and Trafalgar; had been rubbed down quite literally, as far as I was concerned, by the new black boots that had gouged great hollows out of the back of my heels.

To a casual eye, we all looked roughly alike, and all roughly like sailors. We were often mistaken for sailors, in fact, by people who didn't know any better. But Chief Petty Officer Wilmot, of the yellow fangs and the bloodshot and unremitting eye and a voice like a rusty winch, and Petty Officer Trim, who had been twenty years a postman and was not relishing his recall to the colours, would never have made such a mistake; nor would the other Petty Officers who gave themselves sore throats trying to instil into our civilian spines a proper naval erectness.

I suppose they had the same trouble with every new batch of ratings who succeeded in making even the tiddliest uniform look like a civvy suit, and only picked up the bad habits quickly: caps flat-aback, caps full of cigarette ends, jumpers furled like sails. But I can imagine that aircrew under training, such as we were, were more intransigent than most, having joined for flying and not for square-bashing.

Most of us, indeed, kept up the nautical pretence, indulging the licences of language, even rolling a little when we walked. Some went so far as to have their fore-arms tattooed with designs they were likely to regret later;

though most stopped short of anything so permanently committing. In fact, when I paid my visit to the little man in South Street, Pompey, and chose the gruesome but unexceptionable device of a skull and snake (in preference to the Edwardian chorus girls who undulated, or the swallow with a streamer, etched in the crook of the thumb) I went alone. And when, later, I gingerly rolled up my sleeve and soaked off the bloody piece of toilet-paper which is the tattooist's universal bandage, I was mocked for my presumption. "Thinks he's a proper sailor now," was the attitude of those who had no intention of becoming any such thing. Nor, indeed, had I. I only wanted to be tattooed. But no one pretended to believe that.

One or two, wealthier or sillier or merely less adaptable, expressed their forfeited independence in other ways. They garaged their cars in Gosport and went roaring off to London at every opportunity. In between, they spent their time in the more expensive hotels in Southsea.

The rest of us conformed, partly because of the novelty, partly out of apathy, and partly because of unpleasant rumours that if we made too rich a hash of H.M.S. *St. Vincent*, we should never get to flying school. And so we sweated over our morse-sets and the stoppages which the Lewis gun is heir to, and turned out night and morning at the wailing of the sirens. At the end of eight weeks, when we were sent on leave, we would have made rotten sailors, but we were ripe for learning to fly.

II

"I certify that I understand the petrol, oil, ignition and oiling system of the MAGISTER-type aircraft, have been instructed in airscrew swinging and starting up, and have read all local flying orders including A.M.O. A417/37.

Date.............   Signed............"

The purple stamp at the top of the first right-hand page of our brand-new, unblemished, pale-blue Royal Air Force Pilot's Flying Log Books had an air about it, a definite air. It wasn't conspicuously true, of course; and there was no parallel entry on the opposite page to suggest that we had actually flown; but still . . .

We stood about in tense, facetious little groups in the crew-room, surrounded by our brand-new flying-kit; sidcots and quilted linings, gloves, silk inner, wool inner and leather outer, flying-boots, helmets and ear-phones, and a small, clean white kit-bag to contain them.

Outside the window of the nissen hut, a muddy track led up past the hangars to the tarmac and the control tower and the grass airfield. Magisters—"Maggies" already and for ever—were drawn up in a neat row: neat little aeroplanes with a single low wing, two open cockpits, and a wide under-carriage with wheel spats. It was desolate, and rather cold for the end of August, and every now and then a spatter of rain rattled on the windowpanes.

One of the instructors, a Flying Officer in battle-dress and flying-boots, strolled in, and we scrambled to our feet. He looked us over, and his glance came to rest on me. "Right; you're next." As I followed him out, he said:

"Read your Pilot's Notes? Good. Well, there's nothing to it." He walked quickly across the apron to the nearest Maggie. He had a russet, old-young face with a prim little mouth, and talked over his shoulder to me as I panted after him, terrified of missing some vital instruction, while my parachute harness got tangled up in my feet at one end and my Gosport tubes at the other, and sweat sprang out at every pore. Supposing that one did feel sick, or, for some other trivial, unforeseen reason, was considered unfit for flying . . . It didn't bear thinking of.

The instructor swung his parachute easily over the little open door into the bucket seat, arranged the straps and the safety-belt, and turned to me as I struggled up the wing, feeling clumsy and incompetent, and lavishly overdressed.

"I'll give you a hand with that," he said, and took the parachute from me. Soon I was settled and buckled into the front cockpit, and felt I should never move again. His voice came over the intercom, explaining what was happening—"petrol on, switches off, throttle open: suck in"—as a mechanic took the propeller with one hand and casually twitched it over. Of course I knew what it was all about: hadn't I signed the purple stamp in my log-book?

"Right. Throttle closed. Switches on. Stick well back. Contact!"

The propeller was swung again, the engine fired and started, and the little aeroplane shook. My stomach turned over for the first time.

The instructor ran her up, checked the switches, waved away the chocks, and we went bouncing across the grass to the downwind end of the airfield.

"Just leave the controls to me for the moment," the voice said in my ear; and my hands, which had been doing a delicate shadow-dance with stick and throttle, leapt away. But somehow, there seemed to be nowhere else to put them, and as often as I pulled them away, they slunk back, fascinated, to hover helpfully over the controls.

We turned into wind; the throttle moved inexorably forward; the aeroplane bumped and jolted, gathered speed. The tail came up, and the jouncing became perceptibly lighter. The wind began to tear at the edge of my helmet. There was one more bounce, and the surface of the aerodrome seemed suddenly to have become much smoother. We seemed to be taking a prodigiously long time to get into the air. It was very odd.

For the first time it occurred to me to peer over the side of the cockpit. With a sense of limitless shock, of limitless delight, I saw the hangars, the parked aircraft and the figures on the tarmac sinking away beneath us.

[15]

We were flying!

For a moment I forgot all about the effect of controls and the pilot who was using them in the cockpit behind me; forgot even to be frightened as I saw the town with its tangle of streets, its cooling towers, the much-camouflaged Vauxhall works at the bottom of the hill, all fall into plan. The invisible air, flowing over wing and tail, bore us up; and everything that had ever been said or written or dreamed about flying was at that moment acceptable and true.

The stick moved a fraction, the wing dipped, and the world turned gently about our axis. For a second or two the earthbound self protested at the novelty of this; became adjusted; and was prepared to surrender its prejudices and habits to this new element in which it was bird-free to dive and swim and glide and send the meadows spinning.

Above the noise of the engine, the instructor's voice was speaking, and I pulled my mind away from all this abstract exuberance and prepared to concentrate.

"Move the stick forward, and the nose drops. Pull the stick back, the nose rises. Push the stick over to the left . . . all right. You've got her. Just try flying straight and level for a minute."

Well, there was no harm in trying, even if at that instant the machine had acquired a will of its own and now went swaying and yawing about the sky like a . . .

"Don't over-correct. Quite small movements of the stick are sufficient."

That was better. We were flying moderately straight and fairly level.

"You must not keep your head in the office. Look at the horizon."

Guiltily I looked out. The horizon certainly wasn't *there* when I last looked at it.

"Right. I've got her. That wasn't bad."

With resumed and terrifying grace, we swung into a steep turn, the patterned landscape vertically beneath our shoulders. Yes—and there were the hangars, and so that plot of grass must be the airfield. Down, down into the circuit. Now we were coming in low over the boundary hedge, sinking, floating, tearing past the countryside at headlong speed.

With as little warning as they had left it, the wheels touched the grass, and we were on the ground, twice as gross and trammelled for the freedom we had lost.

"How did it go?" Jock asked, as I staggered back into the crew-room with my parachute.

"All right," I said. "Fine. It's rather fun, isn't it?"

"Be all right when we go solo," Jock said. I nodded. Such fearsome responsibilities still seemed many hours away.

III

"Effect of Controls", "Straight and Level Flying", "Climbing, Gliding and Stalling", "Medium Turns", "Taking off into Wind", "Powered Approach and Landing". First page of the log-book nearly filled: rapture formalised.

"Spinning"—underlined in red, and with good reason. We climb dutifully to 3,000 feet, the instructor explaining what a spin is and why it merits a red line beneath it. First, a normal stall: both wings stall simultaneously, the aeroplane has lost flying speed, the nose drops, flying speed is regained. Everything is back to normal. A well-behaved aircraft, like the Maggie, does not spin when she stalls: others, less well-behaved, do. But even the Maggie can be made to spin—like this. The engine is idling again, the speed falls off; she's on the stall now. Now! Stick hard back, hard left rudder. The nose jerks up, the left wing stalls and flicks down—an end of the world feeling, hanging in one's straps, stomach in turmoil, and the landscape swinging over in a terrifying arc—in a second the aircraft is pointing steeply earthwards and spinning round its own axis like a

B   [17]

sycamore seed. The altimeter needle unwinds steadily: we're down to 2,500 feet already; a soggy, helpless feeling. Stick hard forward; hard opposite rudder. Half a turn more and the spinning stops, the speed goes flashing up, and we pull out of the dive at 2,000 feet with ringing ears.

"Spinning"—underlined in red.

The next afternoon I was due to fly again. My instructor saw me and said: "Go ahead and get into the aircraft— P6452. I'll be over in a minute." I humped my parachute on to my shoulder and started off across the tarmac. Two or three mechanics were standing in a group, looking south.

"Must be ours," I heard one of them say. "There's been no warning."

"Silly beggars—trying to put the wind up us."

I looked where they were looking and saw them too: one squadron, two squadrons of aircraft, racing in low down in a long, flat dive. Cutting clean through our circuit, I thought. Cheeky bastards.

They were over the southern boundary now, sweeping straight in across the aerodrome. Showy lot of . . . and at that moment, the first bombs went off.

I was alone in the middle of the tarmac. I dropped my 'chute and started running in the direction of the shelters. The air was shaking with the roar of engines and the explosion of the bombs, and I dived off the tarmac towards the first bit of cover I could see—anything to get off that naked asphalt. As I went flat, I heard a loud crash just behind me and tucked my head well down and waited as Jock and Barry and I had waited on the top of G Block. Waited, and waited—for what? The sudden, felling weight at the back of the skull, for the crack of the exploding bombs to be translated into unendurable pain or oblivion. Waited—until, suddenly, it was all over. I scrambled cautiously to my feet.

"Come on in, chum!" someone shouted at me from the shelters, twenty yards away. I looked at my recent "cover"

—an empty dust-bin and a small heap of sand—and scampered over to the nearest shelter and slithered into it. It wasn't much improvement, a slit-trench covered with a sheet of corrugated iron and a few mouldy sandbags, a foot deep in muddy water.

A labourer in hob-nailed boots made room for me, and in doing so trod heavily on my right foot. I let out a yell, and hoisted the foot out of the mud. It shouldn't have hurt that much. We both looked down at it. The shoe was slit from welt to laces and releasing a rich compound of mud and blood.

"Blimey, mate," said the labourer. "You're a effing casualty! 'Ere," he shouted at the others who were pressed in behind him like pilchards in a tin. "Bloke here's bin wounded!"

"It's nothing," I said. "I didn't even know it had happened till you trod on it."

He laughed heartily at this, no doubt thinking it highly whimsical, and I suddenly felt furious with him, as if somehow the whole thing was his fault.

Down the hill, in the Vauxhall works, the raid was still in progress, and the valley was stained with smoke and flame.

"Looks as if they've finished with us," said the labourer. "Better get you to the ambulance. D'you think you can walk?"

"I've just run twenty yards," I said crossly, "so I should be able to make it." A silly, piddling little thing like a bit of shrapnel in the foot. A bit of sticking-plaster should do it. "I'm all right," I said. "I'll go over to the sick-bay and have it patched up." But by then the M.O. had turned up, and I was firmly escorted to the ambulance and thrust inside. The only other casualty was there already. He had been driving the tractor that towed the old experimental Fairey Battle about when a bomb landed alongside him. It overturned the tractor which threw him off and then landed on his ankle. He was in considerable pain, and groaned and cried all the way to hospital.

We drove out of the camp gates and turned down the lane that led past Vauxhall's and so into the town. A bomb had landed in the works' car-park, and a score or more cars were burning merrily. The huge factory itself, with its camouflage nets and all its elaborate disguise, had had quite a going over, and the road was crowded with fire-engines and ambulances and littered with broken glass and debris. Several fires were still burning, and the whole place had the unkempt look that always goes with bombing, an air of dishevelment and distraction.

The hospital foyer was crowded with the injured, and running with blood. Each ambulance that drew up at the door brought more, to sit holding their pain on the narrow forms or lie writhing and crying out on their stretchers, the girl with her left leg almost severed above the knee, the old man's face shredded by broken glass, the man with his arm crushed into a pulp. And me, with a small cut in my foot!

The staff worked like furies, and within an hour I was led off to a small room full of the colour of blood and the smell of ether. The foot was X-rayed, the wound cleaned and the ragged edges trimmed off with a scalpel and stitched together. Then, as two or three small bones were broken (the news of this made me feel a little better among so much complicated carnage), the whole leg was put in plaster up to the knee.

An hour later I was tucked into bed in a large, bright, comfortable ward, under the eye of an extremely pretty nurse, and lolled back in that supremely irresponsible, spoiled and cared-for feeling which is one of the consolations of being hurt or ill.

IV

The shock came later, with the first air-raid warning that wrenched one's heart into one's throat. But that was merely one of the small private worlds of fantasy and terror that almost everybody knows in war, a terror that has no conscious link with fear of death or fear of pain, but is a cowering of the spirit before the assembled, manifest forces of the dark. It may be recommended as a useful purge for arrogance.

Jock and Barry and one or two of the others came to see me, but already there was a distance between us. They talked incessantly of flying, and I listened enviously; like the banquets of Tantalus, it lay just out of my reach; all the more teasing because I had had a taste of it. Before I left hospital, with my leg still in plaster, on ten days' sick leave, Jock had gone solo, and I knew that I should drop back one course, probably two. Like Housman's condemned prisoner, I stood and counted them and cursed my luck.

I got back to find myself completely separated from my original course and friends—with the exception of Barry, who had also dropped back, through illness—and felt like a small boy who has been moved down a class in mid-term. At first my leg was still in plaster, and I was not allowed to fly. Instead I got a double dose of lectures, only escaping when I managed to persuade the Link Trainer Instructor to let me put in some practice on his machines. It wasn't flying, boxed up in the glowing, airless cockpit, eyes glued to the blind-flying panel, but it was better than nothing.

At last, the plaster came off; the wound was neatly healed; and I limped back with a clean bill of health. A fortnight later, after a final twenty minutes of circuits and bumps, my instructor climbed out of the rear cockpit, made up his straps, shut the little door, and, leaning over to me, grinned and shouted in my ear: "Away you go, then! Good luck!"

Any flying career, however brief or uneventful, has moments that remain fixed in one's memory; moments, too, of greater delight, of surer mastery, but none of sharper sweetness, than the occasion when one has an aeroplane entirely to oneself for the first time. Not that there is very much to be said about it. One taxied out (but with what excruciating care!), took off into wind (but with what concentration!), climbed to 600 feet, made a circuit, and (but with what checkings and re-checkings of trim and flaps, of speed and height!) landed: a series of actions one had performed many times before, and which was not, when all is said and done, very difficult. But oh the terror of it, the unassailable achievement!

First Solo—underlined in red!

V

The nights at Luton were hell—and not simply because we slept in tents on the perimeter of the aerodrome. While I was in hospital, the raids on London had started, and walking back last thing at night we could see the sky to the southward grow garish with ack-ack bursts and the reflected glare of fires. A night-fighter Defiant squadron had moved in on us and stood by to take off from dusk to dawn. We were usually turned in when the cartridges of the Coffman starters went off with that breathy explosion and the engines opened up, one after the other. Lying curled up for warmth under our dew-damp blankets, we would hear them taxi away to the extreme leeward boundary, the sound of their engines growing fainter and fainter. Then we would wait. The field was small and lacked any night-flying equipment beyond two shaky lines of gooseneck flares; and it so happened that the longest run possible brought them straight over our heads. With a certain amount of wind, it was just about long enough; and I imagine that the thoughts of the pilots in the cockpits were very much the same as ours in our beds, only more so.

A burst of throttle as they turned into wind; and then the gradually increasing roar as they came tearing across the grass towards us, louder and louder until they went storming over our heads, twenty feet up. Except one night. The first one came over, very low, and the second. We heard the third, blasting towards us, full-boost, closer and closer. Then there was a tremendous roar and a crash, and the tent collapsed round us. Terrified, half-awake, we fought our way out from beneath the folds of canvas. The tent next to ours was in ruins; and, fifty yards away, wingless, motorless, lit up by the glare of its own flames, the carcase of the third Defiant. Nearby had been parked an old, open Bentley. The Merlin engine, struck from the aircraft, had landed neatly across the back seat, where it burnt itself, and the car, out. The grass was on fire, and the Bentley, and the tent—a scene of vivid, flickering nightmare among the truckle beds and the scattered personal possessions.

Incredibly, it seemed that no one had been killed; neither the pilot nor his air-gunner, nor the inhabitants of the tent which they had sent sprawling. But we did not sleep the more soundly for that.

Shortly afterwards, a soothing rumour spread round that we were to move into Luton Hoo, the vast eighteenth-century mansion set in its park on the other side of the town; and for forty-eight hours or so we were reconciled to our moist bunks in the gathering winter dusks by dreams of palatial splendour. And indeed, we did move to Luton Hoo—but not into the mansion. The truck that took us rolled bravely up the main drive to within crossbow shot of the splendid portico, then shied off into the rhododendrons and deposited us among the sadly dilapidated stables.

The roof leaked and the mist seeped in through the rotting sashes and the trees wept round us and on to us; but the place had a melancholy, mid-winter charm, and—a good point—no aeroplanes took off directly over our heads.

VI

Slowly I became identified with my new course. Jock had gone on, but Barry had slipped back through illness, and saved all situations with some inexhaustible reserve of humour. With his thick, mobile lips and strawy hair already thinned far back off his temples, he seemed a roué of thirty-five against the rest of us. How old he really was, none of us knew. But his talents were immense, the sociable and unfailing talents of faultless piano-playing, a huge repertoire of songs and stories, and, above all, the talent of his own personality. Grouped about him, like a circle of court favourites, were the members of his cast: Tudor Evans, mad, sardonic Welshman who—according to Barry—spent one leave on a dreadful bender in Wales and woke up, at the end of a week, stark naked on the ramparts of Harlech Castle; Mandy Nihill, lank-haired, cadaverous and irredeemably scruffy, wandering through life as if all other clocks in the world but his had just been put on an hour; Michael Holdsworth, tall and fair and incorruptible, with an unvarying gentleness of manner and a vagueness that reduced the instructors and others in authority over us to helpless despair; Robin Lloyd—a special friend of mine—with a face like an uncommitted gargoyle's and a meticulous passion for the music of Beethoven and the poetry of A. E. Housman; John Sayer, as tall as Michael, and as dark as he was fair, firmly braced against a world of falling tents and aeroplanes; Ronnie Martin, with his long, hooked beak of a nose, persistently dew-dropped, and his air of a badly ruffled pelican.

They were the principals; but there were a host of minor characters, Paul, Gouldie, Brian Rose, Nobby Clarke, Nias, Herr Turralbaum. . . .

There were the flying instructors who existed chiefly as disembodied voices issuing out of the rear cockpit; and MacSweeny who initiated us into the mysteries of the .303 machine-gun with an especial relish, a little, thickset, swart man, as black and bitter as a Guinness, forever singing "The Boys of County Cork", who loved to recount how, as a child, he had stood at the window of a house in Dublin and watched a Mills bomb tossed from the floor above land and burst in the back of a truck packed with Black and Tans. The memory of it had coated his character with a dark, impersonal ferocity, and he handled his weapons like an alchemist his retorts or a headhunter his heads.

There were the C.O. and the Chief Flying Instructor, inscrutable behind thickets of moustache. I was standing on the tarmac outside the control tower one morning, waiting to fly, when I overheard a conversation between them as they watched an unidentified aircraft fly quite slowly over the fields a mile or two away.

"By Jove, old boy," said one of them, "that looks remarkably like a Dornier 17."

"No, old boy," replied the other, "that's not a Dornier 17; that's a Blenheim."

"I don't think so, old boy."

"No doubt about it, old boy. That's a Blenheim."

The aircraft slowly circled the town, dropped a load of bombs on a hat-factory, and flew slowly away. A thick column of smoke rose over the flank of the hill. The first moustache turned to the second.

"Blenheim, old boy?"

"That's damned odd. I would have sworn it was a Blenheim."

VII

The weeks slipped away. The entries in the log-book, beginning now to lose that fine gloss, grew from page to page. "Steep Turns", "Instrument Flying"—conducted under a hood like the hood of a pram—"Navigation"—maps bellying unmanageably on one's knee: is that Reading? or Bedford? or . . . ? "Low Flying"—underlined in red. Deservedly. Flying related, not to the invisible air or the changing facets of a cloud but to the particular details of trees and hedges flashing past on a level with one's eyes, the forbidden excitement legalised. "Aerobatics"—the long dive and swoop of loops, the quick disorientation of a roll off the top, hanging momentarily with only two strips of webbing and 3,000 feet of air between one's hair and Hertfordshire. "Action in Event of Fire", "Abandoning Aircraft in Flight"—also underlined in red: remote, unforeseeable eventualities. "Sideslipping"—demonstrated to perfection by the fat, phlegmatic test-pilot in the flying test-bed Battle with its outsize Sabre engine, rolling round the circuit like a porpoise at 1,000 feet, then slipping off his height over the downwind boundary, cutting a couple of earnest little Maggies out of the circuit—blast his eyes!—and dropping her in like a feather.

The hours piled up along the lines of a routine that was never quite, for us, routine. One got hopelessly lost on a cross-country, or flew too low over fields where one was not supposed to be flying low at all. Dusk closed in with one aircraft still in the air and a worried instructor stamped up and down outside the control tower, waiting for him to come sneaking in over the hedge with the last gleam of watery yellow light growing ashy in the west; waiting for the embarrassed phone call—forced landed in a field, sir; terribly sorry, sir; got lost, sir—only the field happened to be, by an odd coincidence, only half a mile from home. The sudden hilarities, as when someone's engine stopped as he was taxi-ing out, and, setting switches and throttle, he nipped out and swung the propeller himself. The engine started, but, unfortunately the throttle was set a little too fast and the aircraft charged him, like a car in gear. He ducked the propeller and managed to grab a wing-tip, while the aeroplane galloped round him, and went on galloping round him until help came.

The long-expected dreads: "forty-five-hour test"—that uneasy quarter-of-an-hour with the No. 2 moustache.

And the end in sight. December 4th 1940. 1600 hrs. Magister R1898. Self. Navigation. 1 hour, 5 minutes.

The last entry from E.F.T.S., and another purple stamp: Proficiency as ab initio pilot. To be assessed: as ab initio: Any special faults. . . .

And the air full of rumours. Every other course had gone on leave, and then to Netheravon, outside Salisbury. We, too, were going on leave; but for us, rumour said, there was to be some other destination. But what?

VIII

We went on leave in ignorance, and instructions to report to the R.A.F. Transit Camp at Wilmslow, outside Manchester, did nothing to enlighten us. Transit—but where?

We trickled in during the winter evening, and reported, one by one, to the Guard Room, to be met by the same question from the perplexed Corporal: "Who the devil are *you?*" Supplemented, for late arrivals, with: "More blooming Fleet Air Arm, I suppose."

We stayed, hating it, for a week.

Then, over the Tannoy: "All leave is cancelled. No member of the draft is to leave the camp."

The 1,000-odd R.A.F. pilots, navigators and air-gunners under training who were "the draft" chirruped like sparrows; but they knew no more than we what was in store for us. We were instructed to label our kit-bags with the curious formula: PETER/SPROUT—a cryptogram that was immediately interpreted into destinations as mutually remote as Northern Rhodesia, the States, Canada, Australia, and—by some unimaginative type—as Peterborough, Northants.

I had caught a stinking cold and sat hunched on my bunk, humid and hoarse.

"What have you been doing?" Barry asked, returning cheerfully from french leave, a good eighteen hours adrift. "Sleeping with a damp woman?"

I felt too morbid to ask him, in return, what he had found to do in Manchester so absorbing that we had had to answer his name on six roll-calls in succession.

At 2.30 a.m. we were turned out of our bunks by a screech from the Tannoy: "All members of the draft fall in outside their huts with full kit and equipment."

Why, we asked each other grumpily, do the forces always move at the hour when man is nearest to death?

The train ambled northwards all day, and deposited us at last on the pier at Gouroch. From there, later that evening, a ferry-boat took us up the Clyde and put us aboard a trooper called the *Leopoldville*. The R.A.F. men were soon stowed away on their mess-decks, leaving the thirty members of the Fleet Air Arm draft, unknown, unwanted, gazing hungrily down into the well of the first-class saloon on to the officers at their supper.

At 11.30 p.m. we were packed ashore to the R.T.O. at Glasgow Central.

At 1100 hours next morning all but three of us were filing up the gangway of the *Leopoldville* which we had filed down twelve hours before. At mid-day she sailed. At 1400 hours, a small motor-boat was discerned haring down the Clyde after us. It drew alongside; a rope ladder was sent down to it; and John Sayer, Nobby Clarke and Nias scrambled aboard.

Being last aboard, we were given the worst possible mess-deck on the lowest possible deck. The ship had been designed for the Belgian Congo run, not for the North Atlantic in December, and she was cold, clammy and uncomfortable. There was nothing to do but huddle about the mess-deck, playing pontoon or poker or reading the few books we managed to borrow or steal—*Twelve Chinks and a Woman* about set the standard—and occasionally poke one's nose out on to the weather decks to blow away the fug. Outside the Irish Channel, it was blowing a gale. For three days we had two other fast troopers in company and a couple of destroyers to look after us. Then one night they left us, and we had the icy grey seas (and any U-boats that happened to be about) to ourselves. In fact, we had no alarms, and the practical discomforts of the weather worried us more than the theoretical probability of being torpedoed.

The conditions were no worse than those on hundreds of troopships—a notoriously incommodious method of travel—throughout the war. Our corner consisted of two long tables running athwartships from the ship's side, and the space above and below. Above, about seven feet from the deck, we slung our hammocks; below we stowed whatever kit we could stuff into the space.

The voyage proceeded uneventfully. We reached beyond the hunting-grounds of the U-boats, and felt the lessening of tension. Rumours of our destination at last crystallised into an official fact: Halifax, Nova Scotia. So it was Canada after all. We accepted it without emotion.

On the weather decks, and on the mess-decks, the temperature kept dropping; and two days later we were alongside the wharf at Halifax, with the bare white hills round us and the dry, keen flavour of a northern winter on our lips for the first time.

The airmen's talk was all of destinations, of Kingston, Peterborough, Picton, Winnipeg, Calgary and points west. They were rattled ashore and stowed into a waiting train by R.C.A.F. officers who knew all about them. We trailed ashore after them, and were still on the quayside when they were snugly tucked away in their carriages, the usual, scruffy, disconsolate little group whose names and ranks and purpose lay outside the sheaf of movement orders.

"Now, how about you fellers?" said the R.C.A.F. Flight Lieutenant, having disposed of the thousand-odd airmen. "Come to take over one of these Yankee destroyers, eh? Well, there they are, boys: take your pick! And God help you!"

[29]

We let out a howl of disclamation, and Barry explained that we had been sent to Canada to learn to fly. The Flight Lieutenant glared suspiciously at our crumpled bell-bottoms.

"Fly! Whoever heard of the boys in navy-blue flying, ha?"

Patiently, very patiently considering how often this had happened, too patiently for a rating addressing an officer, perhaps, Barry told him about the Fleet Air Arm. He listened peevishly.

"Well, for Chrissake, I don't know a thing about that. Who's in charge of your party, anyway?"

"Well," Barry said diffidently, "in a sense, I am."

The Flight Lieutenant looked at Barry for the first time, at his flying-boots, and his greatcoat flapping open, and the long, striped woollen scarf wound three or four times round his neck. "I see," he said. "Don't they teach you people to address an officer as 'sir' in the British Navy?"

"Oh, yes . . . sir," Barry replied with nicely calculated surprise.

"Well, goddammit . . . !" He turned on his heel and stumped away to put through mystified telephone calls to Ottawa. We stood in the snow with our kit-bags (lucidly stencilled PETER/SPROUT) and flapped our arms and stamped our numbed feet. A few fat white flakes floated softly down out of the grey sky and settled on our caps. At that moment we hated Canada with a positive and bilious hatred.

The Flight Lieutenant returned, looking just as angry as when he went, but in a different way. Perhaps Ottawa had made his ears burn.

"Well, Ottawa doesn't know a goddam thing about you either," he said, "but you'd better get on that train—quick! You'll be told your destination at Montreal—when some goon gets his goddam papers sorted out."

The train, which had been hissing and puffing for the past half-hour, obviously itching to get away, was still there.

We hurried across to it, found an empty compartment and scrambled in. One of the airman put his head out.

"The lousy bloody Fleet Air Arm," he muttered. "Always holding up the party."

John Sayer stretched up and removed the man's forage cap and tossed it into the dock. "Mind your manners," he said contemptuously, "you silly little man."

The train was warm, the seats were comfortable; we were out of the snow and out of the *Leopoldville*. We began to like Canada a little better.

No one appeared at Montreal, where we arrived next morning, to reveal our destination to us, and so, for lack of other counsels, we climbed back on board the train and continued our journey westwards. Somewhere along the St. Lawrence valley we happened to meet a journalist from the *Toronto Star*. To our astonishment, he knew all about us; he even knew where we were bound.

"Why sure," he said, "Collin's Bay—Kingston, Ontario. Should be there around half-eleven."

At Kingston, when we finally arrived, there was an open lorry to meet us, and we piled on board.

Was it possible that anything could be so cold? It was nearly midnight. The stars blazed down as if there were no layers of atmosphere to distract their white stare; the flat fields on either side of the road and the road itself stared whitely back. The land, every cup and hollow, every stick and stone, shone stark and clear, and the wind sliced through our clothes. The moisture of our breath froze on our collars and blew away like steam. This was a new world, indeed, polar in its clean outlines and its unremitting cold.

We passed a huge, institutional-looking building set back from the road, and asked the R.C.A.F. Corporal what it was.

"Penitentiary," he said laconically. "Kingston's got everything: pen, looney-bin, military college, P.O.W. camp, university. And it's still the ass-hole of Canada."

Ten minutes later the truck swung in at the camp-gates under the big yellow lamps and halted with a crunch on the hard snow.

"O.K. This is it, boys."

The long riddle of PETER/SPROUT was solved.

IX

From 1,500 feet, the aerodrome was one white field among all the other white fields, separated by a road and a line of fir trees from Lake Ontario which was a white sea, stretching uninterrupted from its shore-side islands far beyond sight to the south and west. The fir-trees petered out along the road to Kingston, being replaced first by a concrete grain elevator and soon by the outlying houses of the town itself. Under the pale, unstained blue sky and a sunlight that hurt one's eyes, such a landscape combined immensity of design and poverty of detail to a degree that baffled, to begin with, senses domesticated by the Home Counties. Once familiar, however, it was seen to have size without grandeur, and indeed a sort of ramshackle domesticity of its own.

The temperature on the ground varied between five and twenty-five degrees below zero, and the snow, packed deep and firm on the fields and roads and on the aerodrome, retained a constant surface, like a skating rink. After the rare blizzards, the new snow was cleared and the surface rolled. Seeing it first, we imagined we should be landing on skis; but in fact it was as hard as tarmac. Only taxi-ing in high winds, when the wheels locked but would not hold, and occasionally landing in bright sunlight, when it was difficult to judge one's height, presented special problems.

The aircraft were Fairey Battles, of venerable age and doubtful reliability, and, since they were no longer regarded as fully aerobatic, a few tinny little Yales in which, with an instructor in the back, we were sent up from time to time to

perpetrate a suitable number of invigilated loops and rolls.
By a curious dispensation—which was later revoked—
Harvards, which were being manufactured in thousands
just across the border and being wheeled across into
Canada, were shipped to England, and Battles from England
shipped to Canada: an uneconomical arrangement since
numbers of each were lost on the double journey, and half
our aircraft were regularly unserviceable for lack of
spares.

In any case, the Battle had little to commend it. At first,
after our trim little Maggies, it was plain terrifying. It was
so vast and metallic, and the cockpit was so charged with
knobs and levers and dials and switches; there was a
retractable undercarriage to worry about, and a variable-
pitch airscrew, both with their warning lights and controls
and gauges, and panel after panel of gun and bomb switches.
Both scale and detail were new and took some getting used
to. Then, after five or six hours dual in the hideous, yellow,
double-humped training version, and a few more solo in the
ex-operational ones, flying them was just plain dull.

We lived in enormous double huts, linked like the letter
H by lavatories and showers common to each, with three-
tier bunks down each side, 120 bunks to a hut. Each hut
was heated by three large furnaces, called Iron Firemen,
that poured hot air out of their innards with a persistent, dry
roaring noise. The windows, which were double-sash, had
never been opened during the winter until we opened them
in a vain endeavour to break the stupefying fug. The effect
was instantaneous. One by one the thermostats got to
work until all three furnaces were going full blast to try
and compete with this unprecedented trickle of icy air; and
the hut grew hotter than ever. After this we gave it up and
resigned ourselves to thick heads in the morning.

After seven weeks, our flying-course, divided into two
unequal parts, was nearly halfway though. We had learnt
to fly an aeroplane; now we had to learn to use it; and so

the routine of turns, navigation exercises, precautionary landings, gave way to formation flying, dive-bombing and firing practice at a towed target. The local flying area was as familiar now as the hills and fields round Luton had been; with the added comfort that one could fly oneself out of the most extravagant navigational blunders by heading due south until one hit the lake shore.

To the north, the country was wild and empty, a forbidding contour map of woods and hills, and lakes fretsawed out of the unvarying snow. One flew over it with mixed feelings. It had a magnificence, a virgin quality, that appealed to any romantic imagination, and which caused one to speculate on one's chances of survival if the motor happened to stop.

To the east of Kingston the lake flowed into the St. Lawrence through the innumerable channels among the Thousand Islands; flowed, in January, invisible and black beneath the solid ice. Where lake and river merged, below Gananoque, the International Bridge went soaring from bank to bank, joining Canada and the States. It was only a short flight away from the aerodrome, and very inviting on a sparkling afternoon with no instructions on one's conscience but "revision". Someone was already boasting that they had flown under its lofty, single span; and, that insidious little voice muttered, if Barry (or was it John, that emblem of virtue?)—why not you? Why not indeed? It would not endear one to the Chief Flying Instructor, perhaps, if he came to hear about it; it would probably mean being kicked off the course, in fact. But—the sky was empty; it would do no harm to drop down and have a look at it. There it was, with a clear run upstream and down: it looked perfectly straightforward.

I flew over it fairly low, turned in a gentle sweep downstream, and headed for it, keeping well down on the ice. From there the space between the bridge and the river did not seem anything like so generous; and the miniature gorge itself seemed to have shrunk to very little more—or even a little less—than the aircraft's wingspan. Simultaneously came the realisation that it was too late to turn away. Hugging the ice and with my eyes fixed on the centre of the span, I pushed the throttle open.

Now I was directly underneath it. I glanced up. There it was, fifty feet at least above my head, the piers of the bridge well away beyond the wing-tips. There was nothing to it, after all. All the same, it was still strictly illegal. I climbed away quickly and hurried back to the local flying area and put in twenty minutes of the most conscientious revision of the whole course. At that I was still sweating a little when I landed.

Robin passed me as I was on my way into the crew room.

"Well, I made it," I said.

"How was it?"

"A piece of cake: room for a vic of three." He nodded; and suddenly a look of consternation came over his face. "Oh Lord!" he muttered.

"What's the matter?"

"I've just remembered. The C.F.I. wants to see you. He rang the crew room a minute or two ago."

My heart quite casually missed three beats. Robin grinned.

"Good luck, chum."

It was obvious. The guards on the bridge had taken the number of my aircraft and had rung up the station. I was done for. Just my luck. I slunk round to his office, guilt in every furtive glance and gesture, my mind babbling over a rigmarole of fatuous excuses. "I just got lost, sir, and found myself flying up the river. I never noticed the bridge . . ." "Bridge, sir? What bridge?" "It wasn't me, sir, I assure you; I was doing revision in the local flying area." "I suppose I must have blacked out, sir . . ." Perhaps I had better faint on his doorstep. . . .

"You wanted to see—er—me, sir?"

"Ah, yes." A pause in which the sun halted in the sky. Then I was impaled on two fierce blue eyes. "Your log-book. Why didn't I get it this month?"

"I beg your pardon, sir?"

"Your log-book, man. I want to see it."

"Oh yes, yes, sir. My log-book. I'll fetch it right away, sir. Now, in fact."

The eyes regarded me ironically. " Thank you very much." And I bolted out of his office, as gay as any re-prieved gallows-man hopping down off his scaffold.

X

We celebrated the halfway mark with our first dose of night-flying. This involved two or three sets of landings with an instructor in one of the dual Battles, and then a number solo. It was not a popular pastime. The hanging about waiting to fly which is so large a part of flying at any time seemed to be intensified at night, and the cold had a still and deathly penetration that settled in one's marrow-bones. The flying it-self made different demands on one's concentration, demands one never had time to take for granted as one took for granted those of flying by day. Imagination, charged with the novelty of the idea, was easily stimulated by the melo-dramatic accessories—the glowing instruments in a cockpit grown suddenly unfamiliar, the purple flames snorting out of the exhaust stubs and the red sparks that flickered away aft as one opened the throttle. It was not difficult, even above that well-lit countryside, to suffer a sudden loss of bearings as one's concentrated gaze shifted from the blind-flying panel to the immense dark outside, a loss of bearings as sharp and baffling as a fainting fit. For a moment the lights of stars and streets became interchangeable, and one was reeling through a topsy-turvy world in which the mind could slip easily from anxiety into blind panic. Only the instruments never lied: altimeter, airspeed indicator, artificial horizon, turn and bank, gyro compass: they inhabited an absolute world, uninfluenced by the tricks of sight or the eccentricities of the middle ear, and night-flying was an absolute submission to their discipline.

There were moments when anxiety was submerged in a brief and splendid exhilaration. The patterns of the town lights, a sky pricked with stars, the surging thought of a continent and half a world spinning through the darkness, and somewhere beyond the edge of sight dawn breaking— one had to free oneself of the link with earth to glimpse these fragmentary beauties, and there, in the end, they were hobbled by responsibilities to speed and rate of climb.

The night's bewilderments played tricks on some eyes. One instructor was drowsing in the rear cockpit while a fairly reliable pupil was doing the last of his dual night-landings before going solo. Everything seemed to be in order. The wheels went down with a jolt, and the flaps. The airscrew whined into fine pitch. The instructor glanced over the cockpit's edge to make sure they were aligned with the flare-path—and grabbed the controls. The pilot was busy making a faultless approach down the main street of Kingston.

"I looked overboard," the instructor said afterwards, "and the first thing I saw was the neon sign on McGall's."

XI

And then, all of a sudden, it was spring. The air lost its cutting edge, the skies clouded up, rain fell; and, almost overnight it seemed, the snow vanished from the earth. Overnight we found ourselves flying over an unrecognisable countryside of brown, sodden earth where yesterday all had been unbroken white. A week later the brown, too, had gone, smothered under a swelling mist of green.

The ice took longer. It cracked first in mid-stream where

the current flowed fastest, the thaw gradually working its way to the river banks and back into the lake. For a time a frill of ice was left, so that from the air every bay and shore and island gleamed with a triple flash of colour; the green of new leaf, the white edge of ice, and the water, kingfisher-blue, between.

Other things had happened to alter the monotony of expensive meals in McGall's and unspeakable meals in camp. We had made friends in Kingston, and I became involved in a tender, rather melancholy love-affair with the daughter of one of the professors at the University. One of the privileges this entailed was that of spending Sunday at their house; and Margaret and I used to watch with immensely superior relish the squabble that invariably developed between the professor, his equally learned wife and their twelve-year-old son—a precocious youth—over the thick supplement of comic-strips from their Sunday newspaper. The pleasures of a private house and Margaret's delicate gaiety and charm made a rare contrast with the sparse amenities of the enormous room.

Barry had branched out in another direction. He had met the people who ran the local radio station—C.F.R.C., Kingston—from a single tiny studio in the university, and had somehow persuaded them into giving him a "Fleet Air Arm Half-hour" to do with as he pleased.

"Oh," he said airily, when I asked him how on earth he was proposing to fill the time, "we'll give them a few songs, crack a joke or two. And, I know, we'll read your poem. And don't you write stories?" Just like that.

Between us we filled five or six half-hours; but as we never received a word either of criticism or praise it was impossible to judge whether the audience—if there was one—enjoyed them as much as we did. I doubt it.

Robin and I spent a week-end in Toronto at the invitation of one of the Canadian pilots in the billet, and visited Niagara on a yellowish, drizzling day at the fag-end of winter, which is a deeply depressing thing to do. And with Michael and Barry we went to Montreal and stayed at the flat of some friends of Barry's, two sparkling sisters rejoicing in the names of Mimi and Jacqueline, their mother and "the twins" who were quite small. Mimi painted, Jacqueline acted, we all talked incessantly and all went dancing at the Mount Royal Roof where the band insisted on playing a particularly silly song of the period—"The King is still in London"—over and over again—perhaps under the impression that it was a revised version of the national anthem —until we collapsed in helpless tears of laughter. What else we did I haven't the faintest idea: only a kind of montage of events and places remains, a vivid nostalgic blur of the trees bursting out all along Sherbrooke Street, and Jacqueline's brilliant, lovely face, and a desperate anguish at the possible sweetness of a world which all the time was slipping through our fingers.

XII

The low dive-bombing, the high dive-bombing, the air-to-air and air-to-ground firing, the formation flying, the navigation tests, the final flying tests, the examinations in ground subjects, were all over. Robin had beaten the record for error in high dive-bombing by missing the target by nearly a thousand yards—an oversight that brought a highly indignant letter from the farmer who had been standing a thousand and three yards from the target. And Barry—dear Barry—had survived landing with his wheels up less than twenty-four hours after the C.F.I. had stated, with considerable emphasis, that the next man who did so would be put on the first boat home. One or two, for various reasons, had gone home already. The rest of us, the Exceptional, the Above Average, the Average and the Below Average—according to our final assessments—had scrambled through as best we might, and were now entitled to put up our wings. We had no wings, of course, to put up; the Canadians who were so perplexed at the thought of sailors flying could hardly have been expected to stock such things, even if their one naval clothing store, in Halifax, had not recently been burnt to the ground.

This conflagration affected us in other ways. We had had no access to "slops" since we were first issued with our uniforms at *St. Vincent* nearly ten months before, and we were reaching a state of complete disreputability which had begun to embarrass even us. Our No. 2 uniforms had long since disintegrated; and now even our No. 1's were stitched and patched and too threadbare to be cleaned, even if we could have spent the necessary twenty-four hours in our underwear. Barry, in a moment of civilian relapse, had had black leather patches sewn over the elbows of his jumper.

And now we were on the brink of departure. Mandy, who in some strange dream of oriental ease, had bought a hookah which was on display in the window of one of the drugstores, and which, for an evening or two he had smoked, reclining on his bunk with the thing reeking and bubbling on the floor beside him, was busy trying to sell it to some sucker in the course behind. To another sucker in the same course—which was largely composed of New Zealanders with their unflagging spirits—Barry and Michael were trying to sell the ancient motor-car which they had bought for $15 some months before.

All of us had begun to look ahead, not in the remote and detached manner of the past four months, but now with a positive, personal hunger. Certain of the things—leave, friends and family—that lay in prospect we could take for granted; one—our individual fate—was still undisclosed. With a few exceptions, we all hoped to go on to fighters, and there was much anxious weighing of the advantages of low-wing monoplane training as against the disadvantages of a "below average" in air gunnery, of a bad pass in navigation as against a good record in high dive-bombing.

The next day, 31 S.F.T.S. was behind us and we were on the train again, heading north and east. Stopping briefly here and there, and long enough in Montreal for Mimi and Jacqueline to respond to Barry's last-minute telegram, it trundled us down the valley of the St. Lawrence, through New Brunswick, and deposited us at last in a clearing in the pine and birch woods of Nova Scotia with the suitably eructative name of Debert. It was a variation on the Wilmslow theme, under a metre of spring mud.

A week later we were slinging our hammocks in "Jock's Box"—the for'ard hold, in fact—of an armed merchant cruiser (A.M.C.: Admiralty-Made Coffin) and had joined a six-knot convoy as its sole ostensible protection. It was cold and uncomfortable, and very much like the *Leopoldville*, and a week out I went down with malaria, a peculiarity I was given to in those days. It was my birthday, and after a celebratory supper of bully beef and prunes and custard (!) I retired to my hammock and shivered and sweated to the occasional rumble of depth-charges ringing against the hull.

I was still shivering and sweating when we left the convoy, anchored in Reykjavik, and were bundled ashore, into a truck, and removed to yet another transit camp, some miles outside. For three more days I lay in a sleeping-bag on the concrete floor of the nissen hut (they didn't run to beds in Icelandic transit camps, which set them apart from the others we had visited), past caring; and then, on a diet of bully-beef and hot cocoa laced with bootleg whiskey, recovered.

The camp was no more than a huddle of huts on the slope of a hill, with a stream, swollen with melting snow, for a bath, and a Camp Commandant who, having been in the R.N.A.S. in the first world war, looked on us with an indulgent eye. "Draw your rations" he said soon after we got there, "and you can do what you like as long as you keep out of the camp till 1700."

Which suited us. There was an enticing range of mountains on the other side of the wide, flat, boulder-strewn valley, and with a tin of bully and a few biscuits in our respirator cases, we went exploring like schoolboys. On one occasion, a couple of us rather over-reached ourselves in attempting to reach the highest peak of the range. We topped the crest and, as we stood shivering in the colossal wind, the sun dropped below the farthest horizon of the land. I looked at my watch. It was exactly midnight.

When we reached camp at 4.0 a.m., having lost our way and forded a couple of rushing icy torrents, we had passed through the two hours of thick twilight which, in mid-May, were all the night there was, and the sky was brightening with the dawn. We roared up the little iron stove and made a witches' brew of cocoa, golden syrup and the last of the whiskey, and stood at the door of the hut, and watched the day come spilling over the naked land.

"So this is what war's like," Robin said. "I've often wondered."

XIII

The next day I was walking along one of the valley roads in the direction of Reykjavik when a soldier, carrying a copy of the local army news-sheet, stopped me.

"'*Ood's* sunk," he said.

"What's that?"

"'*Ood's* sunk."

"The *Hood*? Nonsense. She can't be."

"Says so 'ere. '*Ood's* sunk. See for yourself." I snatched the sheet from him. The first details of the *Bismarck* action, which was still going on less than a hundred miles to the south of us, had just come through. The story was sketchy and incomplete—we heard of the great ship's sinking next day—but it was enough to send speculation soaring; it was enough to explain why we had spent a week kicking our heels in Iceland.

Two days later, we, and two thousand other assorted bodies, were herded aboard an ex-Irish Channel steamer and set off at eighteen knots for home. It was blowing a gale, and the staple diet consisted of tinned bacon that came out of the can in streamers of tepid fat, eighteen inches long. The two combined to provide ninety-eight per cent of the strength with all they needed in the way of an emetic. They were as sick as cats for the whole three days. One way and another it was very like many other channel crossings, only more prolonged.

The seas thudded all day and all night against the rubbing-strake on the waterline, and the hammocks, as thick as the branches of a tree, swayed their unhappy occupants to and fro, to and fro. From some of them, who had been in the convoys ahead and astern of us from Halifax, we heard stories of what we had missed. Our particular convoy had come through without a scratch; theirs had been set upon by U-boat packs, and ship after ship blew up with a roar and a belch of flame in the splitting dark. One tanker spewed out her oil as she went down, and this caught fire and set the whole surface of the sea burning with reeking yellow flame. Survivors from a sinking ship to windward had cut loose the sealed fuselages of Hudson aircraft from the deck and took refuge on them as they floated away. Too late they saw where the wind was drifting them.

The North Atlantic was a place of terror; and we had sauntered through it as unconcernedly as any afternoon trippers crossing from Folkestone to Boulogne on a summer Sunday in peacetime.

At Liverpool we were bundled out of the ship and on to a troop train. It was just such another as had jolted us up to the Clyde five months before; but this time we knew where we were bound, we had leave due to us, and the countryside, fresh and blowing under the mild winds of May, had a charm—and a compactness—it had not had then. We had been screwed up to find a wasteland after a winter of bombardment; but from the train windows, at any rate, it looked much as we had left it, only enhanced by absence.

XIV

We arrived at Lee-on-Solent on a Saturday night, too late to replace our tattered uniforms. We tried to use them as an excuse to avoid Sunday divisions, but the Chief P.O. was adamant.

"You blooming well fall in with the rest of 'em, and leave worrying about your uniforms to the Captain. Cor luv us!"—seeing the roughly-stitched rents across the seat of John's trousers, Barry's elbows—"'e will worry, too, I shouldn't wonder!"

We duly fell in next morning with the rest of the ship's company, a bedraggled little band, exhausted and out at elbows. As the Captain came over to inspect us, Barry turned to me and said in a piercing whisper: "This is going to be good."

It was.

The momentary gleam of surprise at the sight of Mandy's cap (as greasy and battered as any old saucepan without a handle) mounted, changed to bewilderment and outrage as his eyes picked out one patch after another, frayed knees and cuffs, torn silks and collars. He stopped and raked us with one long, incredulous stare.

Then he turned to the Commander and asked, very stiffly:

"And who are these men, Commander? Survivors?"

As an epitaph on our wanderings of the previous six months, it would serve.

XV

The first evening in the wardroom of R.N. Air Station, Yeovilton, combined the atmosphere of a refugee meeting, a mutual admiration society and the first day of term at a new school. We were in disguise, to begin with; and our brand-new uniforms, complete with wings on the left sleeve above the single, wavy Sub-Lieutenant's ring, looked as if they belonged to somebody else. In between squinting at them self-consciously every time they caught our eye, we were busy counting heads. Not many, it seemed, had been selected for fighter-training. Mandy was there, looking like a badly-deformed tailor's dummy, and Robin, and Herr Turralbaum. Barry, Mandy said, was to come; they had met on leave, with Tudor who had dipped the course in Canada and was busy re-mustering as an observer. The others, Michael, John Sayer, Paul and Gouldie, were all at Crail to complete their training as T.B.R. pilots; as were all the rest of the course except for the one or two who had put up special blacks in Canada: for them were reserved the more obscure fates of instructing, drogue-towing and "stooging" of various degrees.

The course, in fact, had lost its identity. For the moment our loyalties were still to it and to each other; but soon—in two months at the most—they would be divided again as we were posted to operational squadrons.

"What aircraft have they got here?" Mandy asked.

"Hurricanes," Herr Turralbaum said promptly, "Fulmars, a few Skuas and two Gladiators." He had been here no longer than we, but he had it all buttoned up. He was explaining the routine in detail when Barry walked in.

"Hullo, men!" he said. "Good leave?—whatever's the matter? Have I got a button undone?"

Mandy recovered first. "Barry, you are a swindler!" he said.

"What do you mean?" Then he laughed self-consciously. "Oh, these. Well, yes. The less said about them the better."

"These" were midshipman's tabs on the lapels of his reefer. Barry, the roué of thirty-five, was nineteen. He had been caught by the rule that pilots who received their commissions under the age of twenty became snotties. The effect on us was as if he had turned up dressed as a Wolf Cub.

XVI

The two and a half months at Yeovilton were the last lap in our training. At the end of that time we were supposed to be ready to join a first-line squadron; and so the flying programme was composed of practice in the skills we should need: formation, camera-gun attacks, dummy deck landings on the aerodrome (known as A.D.D.L.'s), in addition to ordinary flying and a fortnight at St. Merryn in Cornwall shooting at a towed target. On the whole it was uneventful. I got into trouble during the first fortnight by riding a motor-cycle the wrong way round the grass square in front of the wardroom—a crime so odious that I was forbidden by the Commander to keep the bike in camp thereafter. So I sold it and bought an ancient B.S.A. three-wheeler and promptly turned it over late one night after a party exactly outside the Commander's cabin. Fortunately he didn't wake up.

I fell in love once again. Her name was Susan, and she had masses of hair the colour of sea-sand, and freckles, and had started life on a ranch in Argentina, and was then, improbably, a cook in the wardroom kitchens.

I also had my first glimpse of the danger that lies always in wait behind the least eventful hour's local flying. Three of us were sent up fairly late one afternoon on a practice formation flight. I was to lead. The cloud was low, a ceiling of stratus at seven or eight hundred feet, when we took off, but the line of the hills to the east of the aerodrome was clear, and the met. report was fair. We scouted round the local flying area, and found a patch of clearer weather to the north-east where we stayed to carry out our practice. When we set course for base, however, we found that the cloud had settled on the hills, barring our way. We ranged the whole area for a space to creep through, but could not find one; and so reluctantly I called up the other two and told them to keep in close as I was going up through the cloud. We were all as inexperienced as each other, but we had to climb to be able to hear base on the R.T., and we had to climb to clear the hills. I headed for home, and we nosed gently up into cloud.

It's an uncomfortable moment as the ground slowly fades through the loose flying wisps and then vanishes, and there is nothing but the blind white vapour, dense, spaceless, timeless, condensing in droplets of moisture on the windscreen. I climbed steadily on instruments. The others could do nothing but watch my wing-tips and stick close, surrendering their wills to mine. It is a hard thing to do, to obey blindly, mindlessly, against every screaming instinct, in the swimming mist; and first one, then the other, lost formation and disappeared. I called them up: no answer. I called up base: no answer. I was frightened and anxious: they knew we had been on course for home; but would they find it? And when they had lost me, had they been able to transfer their concentration from my wing-tip to their instruments, recovering their bearings in time? I was flying level now, above the height of the nearest hills but still muffled in cloud; and then, ahead and below, I saw a slight lightening, a transparency, the hint of a break. Cautiously I put the nose down. The close texture of the cloud was dissolving into swirling strands and tresses of mist; I caught a glimpse of trees, a field, a barn, blurred and yet seeming terrifyingly close. Too close? It was impossible to say. By the altimeter I was now below the level of the hill-tops; but I should be over them and into the plain beyond—almost over base. Was it a trap? As I broke cloud in a flat dive, engine throttled back, would the flank of the hill come up to meet me . . . that last desperate haul back on the stick and the sagging stall into the trees and the roar of buckling metal and blackness and the smoke swelling up to meet the enclosing mist. . . .

I was out of it, down among the small round hills of Somerset, under nothing more lethal than an overcast evening in June. I circled, trying to get my bearings; spotted a church, a wood, a railway line, and, with utter relief, the airfield. My terrors were over: but what about the other two? Would they find the same break in the cloud and slip down through it? I called them up again. There was still no answer.

With shame and foreboding I flew back to the aerodrome and landed. My instructor was waiting for me.

"What the devil happened to you?"

I told him.

"And the other two?"

"They lost me in cloud."

"You had no business to be in cloud."

"It was right down on the hills." It was still. The firm line between land and sky had gone, and there was only the shifting blur through which I had come. "It clamped suddenly, while we were in the air."

"I see. All right. Did you get them on R.T.?"

"Not a sound."

"We'll tell ground to call them. And we'd better warn the Observer Corps." He relaxed and clapped me on the shoulder. "Don't worry. You got back all right and if they'd stuck to you they'd have got back too." That was what I wanted to hear, but it was thin comfort. "They've probably found a hole somewhere and landed away from base."

I went up to the control tower with him. There was no reply to the R.T.; but that meant nothing. It was usually lousy anyway. There were no reports from the Observer Corps. After a time we went over to the wardroom. We didn't talk much; there wasn't anything that wasn't either futile or superfluous to say.

[48]

After an hour the phone rang. It was the Control Tower. One of them had made a precautionary landing somewhere in Dorset. The aircraft was undamaged; the pilot was on his way back by car.

Some time later the Observer Corps rang up. A Hurricane was reported to have crashed into a hill thirty miles away. It blew up on impact. The pilot, of course, was dead.

So the imagination's nightmare had come true, not for me but for him, in the hoodwinking cloud over the hills. "If they'd stuck to you . . ."—and yet, would there always be a residue of doubt left over after all the acceptable excuses had been made? A needle of self-torment which only the slow friction of forgetting would ever blunt?

XVII

At Yeovilton we were in touch for the first time with our own service, or at least with our own branch of the service. *St. Vincent* had been R.N. and pusser, and Luton and Kingston were both run by the Air Force, for the Fleet Air Arm had no training organisation of its own. This was of no particular consequence, for learning to fly is a fairly fixed process, whoever is doing the teaching and whatever the purpose; but now we began to absorb the individual flavour of the "A" Branch, and to discover what we had taken on. Our instructors were men who had been on a carrier's deck and who had employed in action the particular combination of high spirits and obsolete material which were the naval airman's badge and lot. One of them had had three fingers of one hand shot away while doing fighter patrols over Dunkirk in a Swordfish; an incongruous assignment which was repeated time and time again, in Esmonde's Stringbags hurling themselves at the *Scharnhorst* and *Gneisenau* in the Channel, in the long night dive-bombing trips to Norway by Skua from the Orkneys or in Fulmars flapping hopelessly after the Junkers 88's in the Med.

[49]

The Branch lived under the assumption that the odds in any action would be unfavourable, but I don't think this daunted anyone particularly. High odds and indifferent weapons, if attended with occasional successes, breed a perverse pride in those who suffer from them, or, at worst, a useful fatalism. And, of course, as a service it was still small, and had the intense, compact loyalty of an arm in which the majority of the members know each other. Loyalty, pride and fatalism provide a sound emotional basis for first-line squadrons operating under difficult conditions, and the Branch had all three.

At Yeovilton we were subject to the pull of these things as a force drawing us into the future. As long as we passed the course—and nobody imagined failing it—we were almost bound to be posted to an operational squadron, and we looked forward to it impatiently. At the same time we could regard with reluctant admiration those who admitted quite openly that all *they* wanted was a nice safe billet in a second-line squadron. Such shamelessness was shocking for the dangerous little fuses it lit in one's mind; the reluctant admiration for one, and, for another, the ugly little doubt that that, perhaps, was what one really wanted oneself, only one was too committed to the opinions of one's friends, or the world (or of oneself) to admit it. But at that point not only self-respect but commonsense stepped in to suppress such loose thoughts. They could keep their "stooging". It would be abominably dull. The prospect of flying over-age Rocs and Skuas on endless target-towing trips exercised no temptation on those who had Hurricanes to play about with.

The Hurricane and the Fulmar were our main preoccupation. The Fulmar was the Battle all over again, a two-seater fighter with eight front guns, a large, decorous aeroplane whose only fault was that it was 100 knots too slow. The Hurricane was splendid, very strong and steady, with a clean, purposeful line to it and no vices except a tendency to drop a wing on the stall. Its reputation stood high, and it was the best fighter the fleet possessed. Needless to say, the fleet did not possess very many of them (as the wings didn't fold, none of the *Illustrious* class of carrier could accomodate them), and in any case, by the summer of 1941, the Mark I was already obsolescent.

As a change, we did occasional trips in a Skua, a terrifying aircraft that was as nose-heavy as it looked and was reputed to be impossible to get out of a spin; or in one of the two Gladiators. The Glads were flying of a different era, with their two short wings and tangle of struts, and the breech-mechanism of the two machine-guns—which fired through the propeller—down by one's feet. They seemed uncontrollably light after a Fulmar, and swung like tigers on take-off if they were given their head. One of the pupils at Yeovilton succeeded in turning one upside down without ever getting off the ground.

The summer slipped away in the thick, snug Somerset countryside. Our fighter training was over, and we were transferred from 759 Squadron to 761 Squadron next door for a final fortnight of night-flying and A.D.D.L.'s. Flying over the blacked-out English countryside was very different to flying over the lighted streets of Kingston, but the fortnight passed without incident. By the middle of August, it was all over. We were sent on leave to await posting. But posting, when it came, was not to a squadron but to Royal Naval College, Greenwich, for a ten-days' course designed, as we sourly remarked, to teach us the proper way to hold a knife and fork.

We attended the lectures on naval history and ship's routine, and practised judo with an old Commander of seventy who had muscles like Sandow and delighted in throwing us flat on our backs with a flick of his brawny wrist, and ate our meals beneath the sumptuous bared breasts of the goddesses on the ceiling of the Painted Hall and the fawn's eyes of the waiting Wrens, with a lofty patience which betrayed a sorry lack of historical sense and artistic appreciation.

It was a period that seemed quite isolated from the war; but at the end of it we were jolted back into context. Our postings came through. Mine was to 880 Squadron, then stationed at Arbroath on the east coast of Scotland, whither I was directed to proceed without delay.

Sea-time—H.M.S. *Indomitable*

Sea-time—H.M.S. *Indomitable*

I

THE three-wheeler was at Yeovilton, and so a little guiltily I caught a train in the opposite direction to that in which I was supposed to be going, picked her up, extracted some petrol coupons from the Captain's Secretary, and set off smartly in a north-easterly direction. Since being slow-rolled, she was minus a windscreen, and I donned full flying-kit down to boots and helmet and goggles, for the year had already begun to turn cool. This rig caused a certain amount of alarm and speculation, particularly in the remoter Border villages, and by the time I reached Arbroath, I was growing accustomed to the suspicious glances of policemen, air-raid wardens and other guardians of the public welfare.

"880 Squadron, sir?" said the sentry at the gate. "Oh, they've left, sir. Gone to the Orkneys, I believe. Here, wasn't there another officer in this morning looking for 880? I'll ring the wardroom, sir, shall I, and see if he's still here?"

He was; a submerged, precise little man with the face of an enraged mouse. His name was Jack Cruickshank; we knew each other slightly from fighter school; the disinterest had been mutual. Now he was as fretful as a schoolmistress who lost one of her charges on a country walk.

"We should have been there the day before yesterday," he said, wringing his hands. "I don't know what to do."

"We'll go together in the Beezer," I said, and he accepted the offer with an enthusiasm which cooled a little when he saw her, and rather more when we set off. It was a memorable journey, all the same, through the softest of autumn weather, with the birches shaking their delicate, yellowing leaves like a flame and all the mountains swimming in the liquid, golden light.

At Thurso we put the dusty little machine on to the drifter and, as we nosed out into the Pentland Firth, watched the distant peaks of the Highlands fade into the mist astern. Our destination, we had discovered, was a naval air station with the improbable name of Twatt; and at Twatt—a clearing in the primaeval heather—we duly arrived that evening, just as the bar opened. We were greeted by Moose Martyn, 880's Senior Pilot and a Canadian—one of the laconic ones.

"You the two new boys? O.K. Have a beer."

Half the squadron including the C.O. was at sea in *Furious* on the Petsamo-Kirkenes raid. There was nothing to do but hang about till they came back.

So much we had elicited from him when a seaman came in with a signal. He read it, and then looked at us with a malicious gleam in his eye.

"As you were. Don't unpack, boys."

"Why? What's happened?"

"They want a couple of guys to do a catapult course at Speke. You've never been catapulted, have you?"

"No. Never. But . . ."

"O.K. Catch the plane to Donibristle tomorrow."

"Have you ever been catapulted, sir?"

"Have I hell!"

"But we've only just arrived."

"Never mind. You're going."

We went. Down to Liverpool by air, to be shot briskly off the roaring, flame-spitting, rocket-driven catapult into the Mersey murk, once, and then back to Twatt.

"Hi, boys," said Moose as we trailed back into the wardroom four days later. "Got some news for you. We're on the move."

We sighed, Crooky and I. "The pace of modern life is too much for us," I said. "Where to now?"

"Sumburgh Head. Shetlands. Day after tomorrow."

"All of us?"

"All of us."

It looked as if we were trying to catch the remainder of the squadron up by the land-route. But what to do with the three-wheeler?

II

In the end I had to leave it behind, and a well-intentioned mess secretary sold it to a local contractor for exactly a third of what I had paid for it. The six pilots flew their own aircraft, and the squadron followed with the stores in a Harrow. We had no sooner settled in at Sumburgh than the remaining pilots, Moose, Brian Fiddes, Steve Harris and The Boy vanished. Two went off on an armament course, one on an engine course, another somewhere else, until only Crooky and I were left. Despite the presence of a Blenheim and a Beaufighter squadron on the aerodrome, we were dismayed, and rather flattered, to find we were expected to stand by in case of attacks by German aircraft. We only had 180 hours in, and had never fired our guns in greater anger than is provoked by the average drogue-towing pilot, yet we felt we held the squadron's honour in our hands. Crooky especially. He wandered round with a preoccupied frown on his brow, and I could imagine him practising quarter attacks in his sleep. Dutifully we sat in the crew-room during the hours of daylight, relieving each other for meals, and occasionally being called upon to patrol a convoy of coasting vessels, "far off like floating seeds", moving slowly south and west under the umbrella of one small barrage balloon. Twice we were scrambled and went scurrying off into the sky with our hearts in our mouths on some alarm or other; but on neither occasion was the squadron's honour imperilled by our having to shoot at anything.

The Beaufighter boys were well and truly put in their place while we were there. They had been having a lot of trouble swinging on landing, and damaged so many aircraft by ground-looping them, that the C.O., in despair, asked for an instructor to be sent up to try and put them straight. A day or two later, a Beaufighter duly arrived, made a flawless landing, and taxied over to flying Control. The C.O. had the squadron there to meet it: out stepped a very small, very beautiful, very blonde A.T.A. pilot, on a delivery flight. It was quite remarkable how the squadron's landings improved thereafter.

Sumburgh aerodrome, with the great lion of Sumburgh Head snoozing in the circuit, exercised some incalculable fascination on me. Its sea-circled loneliness, its racing mists and crying gulls, cut clean and painless, like a knife across one's hand.

"These rocks might be the last land's end,
   the farthest bastion
   against the sea's surge and siege. . . ."

It had that feeling of being beyond the world's reach, out on the grey, saga-haunted northern seas.

One by one the squadron came drifting back, and Crooky's and my two-man fighter squadron was re-absorbed. From the positions of C.O. and Senior Pilot (on alternate days), we retired once more to the primitive status of sprogs, the new boys.

Then, in the first week of October, we took off in thick weather and flew back to Twatt, and from Twatt to Inverness; and from Inverness, with the cloud flowing over the hills, Moose took us scudding through the valleys from Falkirk until we broke out, 300 feet above

the Clyde, and so past the black bulk of Arran to the
Mull of Kintyre and Macrihanish.

III

Macrihanish is the Crewe Junction of the Fleet Air
Arm, the uniquely desolate station you arrive at in the
early hours of the morning, wait about at, and finally depart
from, none the wiser. I suppose Crewe has an existence
apart from the midnight fantasies of passing travellers, a
solid existence of Rotary Clubs and Chambers of Commerce
and City Fathers, just as Macrihanish has a championship
golf-course and all the long sea-coast of the Firth of Clyde;
but not for me. Supremely it is the place of departure,
from which one flies to deck-land within the shadow of Ailsa
Craig; an uneasy, queasy staging-point, a bowl in the hills
full of the filthiest weather in the British Isles.

At Macrihanish the remainder of the squadron was
waiting, having flown ashore from *Furious*, and Crooky and
I met the C.O. for the first time. It was a meeting we had
anticipated with some foreboding. "Wait till you meet the
C.O.," Steve had said on more than one occasion, and with
an unpleasant relish. "You won't get away with that with
the Butcher."

"The Butcher", known familiarly as Butch—in reality,
Lieutenant Commander F. E. C. Judd, R.N.—was certainly
unsettling in appearance. He was tall, perhaps six foot two,
and wore a reddish beard and moustache. They require
separate mention, for while his beard was trimmed somewhat after the fashion of the late King George V's, his
moustaches were allowed to run wild. They sprang out
horizontally from his upper lip, stiff, plentiful and coarse,
like a couple of tarred rope's ends in need of whipping. He
was forever handling them; thrusting them up away from
his mouth in a pensive way when he was in good humour;
grabbing and tugging at them when, as was more usual, he

was angry. His temper was volcanic, and his ferocity a matter of legend.

Moose presented us to him in the wardroom anteroom the first evening. He was sitting in a corner, a glass of lemon squash in front of him, reading an ancient copy of the *Tatler* with furious concentration.

"The two new boys, sir," Moose said. "Cruickshank and Popham." Butch lowered the magazine and glared at us with small, unexpectedly mild blue eyes. Then he grunted something unintelligible, but not unfriendly.

"Done any deck-landings?"

"No, sir," said Crooky quickly.

Another grunt. He regarded us for a moment longer, and it was then I noticed his eyes. They were set in skin at once sandy, softly wrinkled and almost feminine, among the surrounding hair, like two pools of shallow water in the lion-coloured African bush. Lost in all that bristling masculine fur, there was something incongruous about them, a softness and uncertainty that did not tally with his manner or his reputation.

"We join the ship the day after tomorrow," he said, to Moose more than to us. His eyes flickered over us, and then he lifted the *Tatler* and went on reading.

"That was Butch," Moose said. "Have a beer."

"I think I'll have a lemon squash," Crooky said.

"And I'll have a scotch," I said. It was borne in upon me that, despite the hesitancy in Butch's eyes, there was trouble ahead.

IV

Two days later we embarked in *Indomitable*, then the newest and largest of the Fleet Carriers afloat.

Because *Argus*, the oldest and smallest carrier afloat, and the ship that did duty as a training-carrier, had been on operations in the exigencies of the time, neither Crooky nor I had ever yet seen a deck. Landing on one was the ordeal that had lain in waiting for us for fourteen months; it was implicit in our choice of service. Without having been through it, our calling ourselves Fleet Air Arm pilots was unsubstantiated, as we had discovered before now.

"What's it like, landing on one of those aircraft carriers?" we had been asked by pretty little things, all agog for hair-crisping tales of pitching decks and hair-breadth escapes. "I can't imagine how you do it."

"Nor can we," we had murmured, truthfully; and watched the look of adoration fade.

Now we were about to find out; and our one idea when we took off and set course over the Clyde was to get it done with as quickly, and with as little fuss, as possible. In this, on our first attempt, we were frustrated by being unable to find the ship; and we returned, the two of us, to Macrihanish with our tails between our legs. Later, after some pointed enquiries from the ship, we took off again, and found her with so little difficulty we could not imagine how we had missed her the first time.

We flew over her in careful formation, and then turned and circled, waiting for the affirmative flag—the white cross on a red ground—to flutter out on the signal boom on the port side and stream aft like a board in the wind. The deck was clear, and we looked down on it incredulously. Were we really going to land on that flat, floating sheet of metal? The idea made no picture in our minds; imagination had no materials to work with beyond the picture that our eyes could see, the long, low, lopsided ship, steaming idly over a grey sea among the hissing rain-squalls.

She began to turn, and as she did so the wake boiled up astern and her speed increased. The steam-jet on the centre-line wavered and began to flow aft. The batsman took his place on the port side by the after 4.5 turrets, a minute, hardly visible figure among all the detail of the ship's side, holding out his yellow bats to us in invitation as we flew past. One or two figures were still moving about on the deck; many more were grouped round the island. As we turned, we looked back. The flag was out. They were ready for us. One after the other, we dropped our hooks.

Crooky, who was leading, put his wheels down and turned across wind. I flew on for a little, and then turned after him in a wider circle; pushed back the hood; lowered my wheels—red lights on, then one reassuring click, and another, as they locked and the lights went off. Wheels down. And downwind now, and the ship in profile racing past in the opposite direction at the tip of an arrow of white water. Crooky was turning in on the last leg of his approach. I put my flaps down, re-trimmed to bring the nose up a little, pushed the mixture control to rich, airscrew into fine pitch, let the speed fall off, following a routine as habitual, as familiar, as tying a tie, yet with the familiarity undermined as in a dream. Under the shadow of this sudden, aching doubt, I began the gentle turn across wind and finally into wind, in line with the ship.

There was Crooky now, almost stationary, poised it seemed over the after end of the deck. Then, with a little bird-like motion, the tail of the aircraft tipped and dropped back. He was down. Two men ran out from each side to clear the wire from the hook, and the batsman, pausing long enough to wave me round, jumped up on to the wing of his aircraft. Words of encouragement, congratulation? Cursing, I opened up and went round again.

What was happening? They were wheeling him aft . . . O Lord! they were making us do more than one landing. I did another circuit and aligned myself with the ship as Crooky sailed off over the bows. Checked my speed: eighty knots. Still too fast. Throttle back a bit. Seventy-five. That's better. Now, where's the batsman? For a moment I can't pick him out. Ah, yes, there he is. And his bats are held level—O.K. I don't seem to be getting any closer; of course, the ship is steaming away from me at twenty-six knots. The right bat goes up and the left one down: looking over the port side, one tends to drop that wing a little. And now, suddenly, the deck is rushing up at me; a glimpse of the thrashing white turbulence of the wake over the trailing edge of the wing; down a bit, down a bit—am I over the deck yet? A fraction of a second of blind disorientation—and the cut. I chop back the throttle, keep the stick central, we're dropping like a brick, a touch of motor, and the quick hard bounce as the wheels touch, and, at once, the jerk of the wire that throws one against one's straps, the tip of the tail, and back, with a soft little thump on to the deck.

For a second relief dizzies me. Then the aircraft is being pushed back; a Petty Officer, leaning against the wind, waves his arms for the brakes and I jam them on and lock them. Someone taps me on the shoulder; the batsman, clinging on to the side of the cockpit.

"That was all right," he shouts, "but watch that port wing. You tend to drop it. O.K.?"

"O.K."

"One more good one then."

He hops down. Quick cockpit check, and he is holding up the green flag. I give him a thumb; he waves the flag; open up against the brakes; the flag drops; off brakes, and we're away up the deck, past the island, a bump as the port wheel rides over the catapult ramp, and into the air over the bows. Round again for a second landing.

This time I ended up well over on the port side and saw myself, for one breathless instant before the hook caught, going over the side. But all was well, and the Flight Deck Petty Officer signalled me up the deck and on to the for'ard lift. Switches off, magnetos, petrol, radio; unlock the straps and throw them back; snap the release box of the parachute, and step out of the harness, over the side of the cockpit on to the wing, to be almost swept away by the hard, flat blow of the wind. My rigger, who is on his way up to take my place, grabs my arm and grins.

"They was all right, sir. Mr. Cruickshank's too. Both very nice, sir."

I mutter something, and scramble down the wing on to the deck, and look round. How bare and bald it is, with the wind tearing over it, and splinters of rain and spray in the wind. There, by the door into the island, is Butch, one half of his vast moustache blowing across his face. I'd better report.

He glares at me through a screen of wind and hair with those uneasy eyes. "Feel all right."

"Fine, sir."

A grunt. "Second one. Over to port. Must keep straight. Give you, Cruickshank, some more." He frowned and grabbed his flying moustache and with a look of indescribable ferocity muttered: "But not bad. Report to Commander Flying." And strode off down the deck.

First deck-landings—but no longer do we deign to underline such red-letter days in red.

v

At first it is all utterly baffling. The ship is so huge, and her geography so complex. One is continually losing oneself, drifting into seamen's mess-decks, or the galleys, full of shining ovens and sweating cooks in soiled white aprons, or reaching dead ends, chilly metal corners smelling of potatoes, and lobbies smelling of hundred octane, facing time and time again the dilemma of the two alternative watertight doors and half-afraid to take off the clips—for fear of what? Of not being able to clamp them on again, of somehow endangering the ship, of being thrust back by a rearing wall of green water. . . . Any fantasy can sweat coldly to birth, like a mushroom, in those long, lit, empty, echoing, iron corridors. And the roaring air is electric with half-heard orders and shrill with bosun's pipes, and brassy with bells and bugles.

Then, gradually, a pattern begins to emerge. The essence of the ship, her brain and nerves, are housed in the island. Tucked away on the starboard side, streamlined, threaded with narrow passages and steep metal ladders, it contains the Compass Platform from which the Captain handles the ship; Commander Flying's position, a narrow gallery with an uninterrupted view of the flight deck; the Admiral's Bridge, the Fighter Direction Office, the Air Operations Room, and the Signal Bridge. It embraces the funnel, and supports the radar aerials, and contains, besides all these, the Pilots' Ready Room, the hot little box with one scuttle which is our refuge when waiting to fly.

The armoured table-top of the flight deck runs away for'ard and aft. It is bare but for the arrestor wires and the barriers that traverse it, and the innumerable ring-bolts for lashing down aircraft. Surrounding it for the greater part of its length are the nets, narrow walkways below the level of the deck-coaming where the flight deck party crouch out of the wind and where all manner of equipment from fire-extinguishers to chocks lives, or is slung. Here, on the port side, the Batsman has his perch and screen, and the Flight Deck Engineer his controls for raising and lowering the wires and barriers. The nets terminate fore and aft with the twin turrets of the twin 4.5's, the ship's main anti-aircraft armament. The tops of the turrets project a foot or two above the level of the deck.

There are two lifts. The for'ard is the only one big enough to take a Hurricane—and then only athwartships—and communicates with the upper hangar, which we share with the Fulmar Squadron and one of the two Albacore squadrons. The after-lift serves both upper and lower hangars. The upper hangar runs the length of the ship from lift to lift, a hollow-echoing steel box which is the headquarters of the squadrons' non-flying activities. It is garage and workshop, with points for petrol, oil, compressed air and power for the tools; and about it, through innumerable watertight doors and lobbies, are grouped the endless cubby-holes that ships and squadrons need for their well-being: squadron stores, battery-charging rooms, blacksmith's shop, paint-store, dope-store, bosun's stores, engineering and electrical workshops and the squadron offices. It is two full decks high, and among the arrestor gear machinery in the deckhead are sprays that can flood it from end to end in case of fire. Spare mainplanes and propellers are clamped to the bulkheads like trophies.

The aircraft are parked, almost touching; the Hurricanes in echelon up the starboard side, the Fulmars up the port side, and the Albacores with the whole of the after end to themselves. To prevent them getting adrift, they are chocked fore and aft and lashed down with wire lashings. These are so arranged that it is almost impossible to take more than three steps without tripping over one. The air has a dead, flat taste, and stinks of oil and petrol; and this smell, a sickly, cloying smell, seems to condense on to the metal surfaces of the deck and the aircraft and the tools in a tacky, black film.

This is where the maintenance ratings, fitters, riggers, electricians and radio mechanics, spend most of their time.

Amidships, one of the watertight doors leads out through a lobby and a second door to a ladder up to the island; and another, aft, down to the cabin flats and the wardroom. Others give access to the weather-decks where the ship's boats are stowed, and there there is fresh air and the sea sluicing past and the paintwork carries a bloom of salt.

The hangar and the flight deck and their appurtenances are the domain of the Air Department; they take their shape and situation from the ship, but their function and character from the aircraft. Only on the Compass Platform, or among the capstans and cables on the enclosed fo'c'sle under the for'ard round-down, on the narrow, cluttered weather-decks or on the quarterdeck with its bell and brightwork and gratings, right aft and far below the flight-deck, where at twenty-six knots the vibration makes one's teeth chatter, is the ship's other essence expressed. It is there, nevertheless. For before she is a floating aerodrome, she is a ship, with the beauty of a ship, and a ship's particular, apprehensible character.

This, like the complex pattern of her lay-out and organisation, it takes a little time to realise. It would come during the working-up period which was now beginning. The squadrons were on board, and a couple of days later the ship left the Clyde with an escort of two destroyers for Bermuda and the still-untroubled waters of the Caribbean.

VI

We headed round the north of Ireland and thumped straight into a full sou'westerly gale. The seas broke over the flight-deck and buckled a sponson or two on the weather-decks and standby was relaxed. The ship pitched and jarred, and many of the company who were still on their feet looked very green about the gills.

Then, four days out, with the weather still dirty, there was a Focke-Wulfe scare, and a Fulmar was flown off the wet and reeling deck against contingencies, and failed to return. Night was closing in when all hope of its finding us through the lowering rain-squalls faded. Darkness fell, and the ship reduced speed, returning to the area at dawn and flying off a team of Fulmars and Albacores to search the three or four hundred square miles of wallowing, empty sea in which, perhaps, pilot and observer were tossing in their rubber dinghy. On the flight deck, squadrons and ship's company gathered, peering anxiously at the long swells that rolled away to the westward.

At last an R.T. message was received from one of the Albacores: the dinghy had been spotted: its two occupants had waved. The ship altered course; and an hour later it was sighted by a look-out on the island. Then we could all see it, as it rose momentarily on the crest of a wave, to vanish again in the trough. On the heaving face of the water, it was unimaginably tiny; and its brief, sporadic and insignificant appearances on the wave-crests were a cruel restatement of man's proportion to the world he rules.

VII

It was some time before the two halves of the squadron knitted in our minds. Moose we knew with his flat, bony face: in the air he was first-rate; in the wardroom, laconic; and with Butch he used a kind of self-contained cussedness that was near contempt. Butch's histrionic furies left him cold, and he showed it with the slightest shrug of his shoulders, a pointed inattention. Brian Fiddes, my flight leader, we knew too; a tall, flexible, rather foppish-looking chap, with strawy hair and protuberant, pale-blue eyes. His voice matched his appearance; it was affected, blasé, the instrument of an amused indifference, and he limited its use to the stock phrases of our trade. "Never a dull, old boy" described everything from a near-miss by a bomb to a raspberry from the C.O. or a barrier-prang: "Pay no regard" might have been blazoned on his escutcheon. It took time to realise that he parodied himself, for he was R.N., and there was something impersonal in his studied fatuity; to realise that he used the formulas of speech and accent to conceal, equally, professional competence, and the deeper springs of warmth and humour. Steve Harris we knew, a flashy pilot for all his bloodhound-look and almost imperturbable good humour; and "The Boy", rich, spoilt, slovenly and usually late, a sheaf of unimportant vices carried with disarming and ruthless charm. We shared a cabin; and on the rare occasions that he used a toothbrush or a hairbrush, he used mine, yet one suffered even this.

And now there were the others; first among them, Dickie Cork, with a D.F.C. and seven or eight confirmed, gained while flying on loan to the R.A.F. with Bader at Duxford during the Battle of Britain. Dickie, the only one of us with fighter experience, had the quality men follow. An immaculate pilot, with the working of the squadron on the deck or in the air at his finger-tips, he moved with the radiance of the Head Prefect about him, taking the worship of the lesser fry for granted and joining in their sport with a certain well-disguised condescension. He treated Butch as if he were a woolly, temperamental housemaster; and no one ever saw him drunk. Johnnie Forrest, a rugger player of note, shared something of the same indestructible boyishness, the same inbred ability. He would be Head Prefect one day: you could put your money on that. Jack Smith and Dickie Howarth, R.N.V.R. to the bone, were of a different stamp. Jack, a geologist by inclination, regarded life and his fellow men with a mature irony, almost as if they would one day be good for classification in a textbook of tolerable fossils; and Dickie, short and saturnine, was the squadron's licensed clown. He had Butch's indulgence, which he abused, and capered as he pleased.

These eight, with Butch, were the squadron's more or less seasoned core, with Bungy Williams, our one P.O. pilot, who lived a shadow life outside the precincts of the wardroom, and had known Butch in Walrus days at Lee-on-Solent, and hated him implacably. And bringing up the rear were Crooky and myself, a serious-minded two-ringer R.N., new to flying, named Lowe, and Paddy Brownlee, an Irishman, gifted to the full with that predilection for abstract conspiracy which is the climate of his race.

In the wardroom, as in the air, the squadrons tended to retain a kind of loose unity, mingling at the edges with friends in other squadrons, yet tending always to re-form, as if the aeroplanes we flew had a limiting effect upon our sympathies. Jock, with whom I had watched the bombs come tumbling down from the roof of G Block, H.M.S. *St. Vincent*, was in one of the Albacore squadrons and we were constant companions at the bar and the shove ha'penny board. He had a gifted bawdiness, a spontaneous disrespect for pomposity and insincerity and humbug, that were refreshing after the prim good manners of my tribe. And there were others; Jack Pike and his observer, Colonel Brown; and Charles Gordon with his yacking laugh, his recondite Yiddish anecdotes, and a library that contained Kafka and Joyce and B. Traven—a private, forgotten world beyond the interminable "shop" of flying.

Everyone had his private world on which his squadron personality fitted like a lid. For weeks or months the lid remained in place, and then, in an odd, unpremeditated moment, would fly off, revealing the most sentimental of lovers beneath the chilliest of Lieutenant Commanders, revealing beneath the most humourless and precise the man who, on the Petsamo raid, packed into the back of his Fulmar a week-end suitcase and his violin, upon the expectation of being shot down.

VIII

At Bermuda, Butch pronounced that all members of the squadron should fly a Walrus. Only Bungy was excused. "You won't get me into a Walrus with the old bastard again," he said with feeling. "He hit me on the head with the stick last time." An improbable story until one learnt that there were two pilots' seats side by side, and one control column that could be fitted in front of either simply by lifting it out of its slot.

We approached the ordeal with some trepidation; but nothing so bizarre happened to us. In fact, Butch, working off on us his nostalgia, was at his most genial; and it was rather fun, taking off and landing on the silky blue water of Hamilton Sound. Then, from Bermuda, at the end of October, the ship proceeded to Kingston, Jamaica, which was to be our base during the working-up period.

The harbour at Kingston is protected, indeed almost land-locked, by the long spit of coral known as Palisadoes. A ship entering the harbour moves along the channel with Palisadoes to starboard to the far western side of the bay. The town, partially visible over the low breakwater of land, passes from beam to quarter; and just at the point where head-on collision with the farther side of the bay seems imminent, a break is revealed. The ship turns tightly through ninety degrees, through perhaps one hundred and forty-five degrees, and now inside the protecting arm of Palisadoes, steams back on her tracks across the lagoon towards the town.

I was in my cabin, changing, when we began to perform this protracted ceremony of arrival for the first time. I had seen glimpses of the white town beyond the reef of green, the mountains and the mountain-shadows under the trade-wind clouds, and had decided to slip quickly down and clean up, in case there was shore-leave. I should be up on deck again before the ship had rounded the tip of Palisadoes.

My mind, or simply my body, perhaps, recorded the heel of the ship as she swung into the outer channel, the sudden drop in engine revs. That was normal, a reduction of speed to four or five knots as we coasted along the shores of Palisadoes towards the harbour entrance. In half an hour we would be at anchor off the town.

The ship was quiet. The ripple of the bow-wave was louder than the throbbing of the engines, and the fans kept up their constant hum through a silence instead of through the normal noises of the ship. Even after an uneventful day of exercises in sight of land, there was the unmistakable feeling of ease and relaxation which comes with the end of any voyage, however short.

I changed quickly. I should just be in time to watch our arrival off the town. Then there was a crash and a shudder, and my chair shot along the floor and fetched up, with me still in it, against the wash-basin. I jumped up, but for perhaps two seconds did nothing but stand, holding on to the edge of the upper bunk, waiting for something else to happen.

Nothing did.

Outside in the passageway there was a babble of voices. "A tin fish!" "Couldn't be. There aren't any U-boats over this side." "What the hell, then? We must have hit something." "Perhaps we're aground." "Oh, my God!"

I dashed out of the cabin and joined them, and we scrambled up to the flight deck by the shortest route, a sick feeling of apprehension working in the pits of our stomachs. At first everything seemed normal, except for the fact that the ship was stationary. She was on an even keel; to port there was only the bland blue surface of the Caribbean and the sloop that was wedged firmly on the coral. To starboard lay the green harbour wall of Palisadoes and the mountains beyond. What on earth had gone wrong? Up for'ard a group of people had collected. Among them were the Skipper, the Commander, the Navigator, the First Lieutenant, the Engineer Commander, Commander Flying, and, of course, Butch. It behoved junior sub-lieutenants to keep clear, and we made our own speculative little groups, peering over the side to see if we could diagnose the cause of the trouble.

After a time, Dickie Cork joined us.

"Well, we're on the rocks, chaps. Thank God I'm not the Pilot!"

"But how? What happened?"

"Lord knows. But it *looks* as if we've been trying to pass the port side of a port-hand buoy. I'd always heard there was no future in it."

He was perfectly right, as always; but that was only half of it. The facts, when we were able to creep up for'ard and verify them for ourselves, were almost too ludicrous to be believable. For, peering straight down from the overhang of the flight deck, we found ourselves looking at the top of a coral reef, nowhere covered by more than a couple of feet of water and in places pushing its fronds of weed and rock above the surface. We could see small coloured fish darting about among the sea-fans, and the blue-black quills of sea-eggs in the crevices of the rocks; and we could not believe our eyes. It was as if the whole vast ship had been lifted up by some unimaginable tidal wave and deposited like a raft on top of the reef. We lay on the sloping curve of the round-down, craning out far enough to be able to look back and down at the stem of the ship; and suddenly all was plain. Through the clear water we could see the edge of coral stopping abruptly and dropping away vertically into deep water, and the ship's bow wedged into it like an axe into wood.

"Blimey," said Jock, heaving himself up the slope on to the flight deck on his belly. "Made a proper job of it, haven't we!" It was not difficult to credit the tale that the leadsman in the chains had swung his lead an instant before the impact, and that lead and line had been nipped between the ship's stem and the coral.

"But how? How did it happen? It's too fantastic." The same question was on everyone's lips.

"There's a buzz that the buoy was out of position," said Crooky, who had joined us. "I don't know if it's true or not."[1]

No one knew. But already the deathly stillness was broken as the engines raced full astern, and the wash boiled up along the hull. The whole ship shook, but after twenty minutes there was no sign of her shifting, and the turmoil subsided. The loudspeakers crackled: 'D'ye hear there!

[1] It was not true.

D'ye hear there! Clear lower decks! Clear lower decks!"
In a short time every officer and man off watch was mustered
on the flight deck, and the Commander and the Master-at-
Arms herded us all aft and gave us our instructions through
a megaphone. The Marine Band struck up; and to the
regular thump of bugle and drum, and to the accompaniment
of a certain amount of ribaldry, the entire ship's company
bounced rhythmically up and down, up and down. Beneath
our feet the armoured deck trembled as once again the
engines opened up. But the antics of fifteen hundred men
shook it no more than they would have shaken the living
earth. The ship remained fast. The sun went down in
splendour behind the mountains, and night mercifully
shrouded our humiliation.

Humiliation it was. Underneath the quips about being
back in Liverpool for Christmas, we all felt the slow smart
of shame, for after six weeks, we were already beginning to
identify ourselves with our ship. *Indom* was our ship—
though we might never openly admit it—and what happened to her happened to us. It was admitted tacitly in the
gloom that settled on us that evening, a gloom that owed
only a little to forfeited shore-leave. There was uneasy talk
of what might be involved if all the immediate efforts to
shift her failed; of emptying her of oil-fuel and petrol, of
stores, shells and torpedoes, and, of course, of aircraft, of
stripping her of turrets and guns and heaven knows what
other things that were points as fixed in our thoughts of
her as milestones along a familiar road. There was much
speculation, also, as to how much damage she had suffered.

Divers were already at work, surveying the embedded
bow, and the few ships that were in harbour were standing
by, ready for the attempt to drag her off. But when we
turned in that night, it felt as if we might remain impaled
there for ever.

Next morning I went on deck, and it seemed as if I must
have dreamed the whole sorry affair. There we were,

swinging gently at anchor off the Aquatic Club Pier. Then the full meaning of it smacked me, and relief swelled up into jubilation. We were off! Some time in the night the combined efforts of our own power and our makeshift tugs had dragged her bows out of the coral, and quietly in the dark hours, we had crept into port. Now we rested placidly on the surface of the lagoon, trying hard to look as if nothing had happened—nothing at all.

For forty-eight hours after that, rumour went wild. As always, whatever arguments developed were based on premises that were, at best, a system of vague probabilities, and at worst faulty guesswork. No one had known before it happened where we were bound, once our work-up was complete: opinion was about equally divided between relieving *Ark Royal* in the Mediterranean, and joining the Far Eastern Fleet at Singapore, with the odds slightly on the latter. But now all the oracles, the seamen's mess-deck and the Captain's Steward, and the key-board sentry who had seen someone hand someone else a letter and he hadn't been able to see the address properly but it was definitely Liverpool, all were equally flummoxed. Then, abruptly, we sailed; and the Skipper came over the Tannoy and told us that we were bound for the Navy Yard, Norfolk, Va., at our best speed, for repairs.

This was later amplified to the effect that all squadrons would fly ashore to the Naval Operating Base and continue their working-up programme while the ship was in dock. Those who had been to the States, and those who had not, were equally delighted.

IX

The arrival of the squadrons at Norfolk created a sensation, and, in the minds of the aerodrome staff, a suspicion, that we never quite lived down. Faced with the enormous concrete runways, of a length and breadth found in England only on the largest bomber stations, the Albacores, Fulmars and Hurricanes landed in formation, two and three abreast, and so close upon each other's tails that there were eight and ten aircraft on the duty runway at the same time. This was too good a chance to miss; it was also good carrier-practice in backing-up. The Americans, who observed the strictest regulations in the circuit, were flabbergasted, and we heard picturesque stories afterwards of the turmoil into which the Control Tower was thrown by this impetuous and highly irregular invasion.

Everything about us and our aeroplanes conspired to baffle the Americans with their rows of silver Wildcats and Douglas dive-bombers. Our shabby sea-camouflage of buff and blue, the Albacores with their two great planks of wings, Butch and his whiskers, all caused them amusement, spiced with an unspoken scorn. "Gee, what an outfit!" they seemed to be saying. "Look at those biplanes, will ya! D'you wonder they're losing the war?"

The balance was partially redressed during the second afternoon when one of their Wildcats swung on take-off and went careering along a line of parked Fulmars, bending propellers and engine cowlings and mainplanes on its way, and finally came to a shaky and lop-sided halt in the midst of them. At least, we could feel, we didn't do that sort of thing.

Their implicit contempt at the apparent mess we were making of the war was combined with a certain amount of loose, explicit boasting about beating the Japs with one hand tied behind their backs. On the latter we had no data (nor had they, but that was a different matter); and on the former, the presence of both *Illustrious* (damaged off Malta) and *Formidable* (damaged off Crete), refitting in American dockyards, provided arguments that were difficult to answer convincingly. And then, two days after we arrived, *Ark Royal* was sunk, almost within sight of Gibraltar; a major blow to the navy's carrier strength, and a personal loss even to those of us who had never known her. She had been the symbol of invulnerability and jaunty courage, the queen of carriers working without harm—despite the fatuous rhetorical questions of Lord Haw-Haw—in the narrow seas which had already seen the wounding of the other two. Her loss made our misfortune off Palisadoes seem more ill-fated and untimely than ever, and our defence of Great Britain's war policy (with the obvious jibe always remaining unsaid) less convincing than ever.

The camp was a vast and terrible place, a city of Quonset huts several miles in extent. A camp-bus service connected its various component parts, but it so happened that when one actually had to make the journey from, say, the bunk-house to the hangar, a bus had always just left. It was the only constant thing about that bus service, and so we plodded stickily to and fro in the baking autumn sunshine, and wished ourselves back at sea.

Our shore-going was perfunctory and unenthusiastic. Norfolk, and Newport News across the sound, were sailors' towns, an overpowering medley of eateries, niteries, danceries and chop-suey joints. Only The Boy, consulting his address book, found a millionaire or two in the vicinity with whom he could indulge his tastes for large meals and the jeunesse dorée. One week-end, Johnny, Steve and I hitch-hiked up to Washington, and gained a fleeting impression of that stuffy, crowded, well-ordered white city, an impression which was largely washed away the following evening by a party on board a ship in the naval dockyard at Baltimore.

On the base itself, our ten days did not pass without misunderstandings. Butch, whose language over the R.T. was never confined to the stilted phrases of the R.T. Code, excelled himself in the miasmal air over Norfolk. He landed after one particularly blasphemous trip—the object of his especial wrath had been me—to find all the telephones in our temporary squadron office ringing themselves into a frenzy.

"They're for you, sir," said the quaking squadron writer, offering him a sample receiver as if it were a live high-tension cable. "This one's the Adjutant, sir."

Butch thrust back a frond of moustache. "What does he want!" He grabbed the receiver and said grumpily: "Yes, yes. Judd here."

The voice from the other end, vibrant with indignation, could be heard all over the office.

"Commander, were you in the air just now?"

"I was, yes. Why?"

"Were you using obscene language over the Radio Telephone?"

Butch bristled. "I may have had to swear at my bloody-fool pilots once or twice. Why, were you listening?"

"I wasn't," said the voice, rising to a crescendo, "but the wives and families of half the fliers on the station were listening. It is their practice to tune in to the various squadron channels on short wave."

Butch chuckled. "Well, what do they expect. This is a fighter-squadron, not a girls' school."

"But, Commander, you don't understand. Language like yours has never been heard over the R.T. before. They were horrified. My telephone hasn't stopped ringing in half an hour."

"Tell 'em not to listen," Butch said, and rang off.

It was remarked, however, that although he still did not restrict himself to the code, Butch purged his language to some extent while we remained at Norfolk. An interview he had with the Commanding Officer of the base may have had something to do with it.

X

It took the dockyard ten days to repair the stem; the squadrons re-embarked, and the ship returned to Jamaica to resume her interrupted work-up. A little time after this, while doing deck-landing training, I had my first crash.

It came out of the blue, as such things always do, and was the result of plain bad flying. At the end of my second approach—Crooky and I were supposed to be doing three landings each—I let the speed fall off and dropped a wing. I smacked on full throttle, but it was too late. The aircraft stalled and hit the rail at the extreme after end of the flight-deck, below the curve of the round-down. People watching expected it to drop back into the wake of the ship. But instead, it had just enough forward speed to slither up the round-down on its belly and come to rest with a grating of torn metal and clouds of smoke and steam on the first wire.

I sat there for a second or two, quite unhurt, with the fumes of petrol and glycol swirling round me. I was far too appalled at what I had done to move. Then someone jumped up on to the wing and started to undo my straps, and I clambered out, prepared to drop the two or three feet to the deck. But the wing and the deck were on a level: and it was then, I think, that the full impact of it struck me.

I was surrounded at once, by the fire-fighting party, the M.O., the rest of the squadron who had been watching, Commander Flying—and Butch.

"All right?" he asked, rather more gently than I expected. I realised I was far more frightened of what he would say than of the crash: I was five, and had broken the mascot on my pedal-car by wilful disobedience. I felt as guilty as sin, with those pale, equivocal eyes on me.

"Yes," I said; and added: "I'm very sorry, sir."

Butch thrust at his moustache. "Never mind about that. Give you some A.D.D.L.'s; you'll be all right." He turned away and started to discuss the question of salvage with the squadron Chief Petty Officer. I had got off lightly: I had expected to be made duty boy for a month at least.

Even Commander Flying dropped his normal crispness. "Pilots are more important than aircraft," he said when I reported to the bridge. "As long as you don't go bending yourself, I don't mind how many aeroplanes you bend." I suppose I should have thanked him for the reassurance, only I didn't quite believe him.

The aeroplane was undoubtedly "bent". The cockpit was intact, and the tail-unit; and that was all. The engine, having been used to drag the aeroplane up the deck—the propeller had made great weals in the metal of the round-down, and one blade had flown off and landed at the batsman's feet—was shock-loaded to the limit; the undercarriage had gone, of course; and both wings were badly buckled. It made me feel slightly sick to look at it.

"What're you worrying about?" said Jock over the gin I had bought him later that evening. "It was a good landing."

"A good landing?" I queried.

"Certainly. You walked away from it, didn't you?"

Much worse than the crash was the prospect of the first deck-landing after it. The shock of a prang, whether one is hurt or not, is to the imagination, which is stimulated into orgies of foreboding. Flying is changed from being an occupation with a high theoretical risk into an occupation the one inescapable end of which is that racking screech of torn and buckling metal. Imagination with such a territory to explore goes mad, reconstructing the events over and over again with gloating relish. If it has too many, either of its own or other people's, to feed on, and if its grisly exercises are not resolutely ignored, it leads straight to that state of jangling nerves known laconically as "twitch".

Twitch of a common everyday kind was common enough; it is as familiar to cricketers waiting in the pavilion or candidates for jobs sitting in waiting-rooms as to pilots strapped in their cockpits on a flight-deck: that slight discomfort in the bowels; occasional fits of acute depression; a racing pulse—symptoms that vanish as soon as there is something to do. But stressed too far, by prolonged periods of operations, by a run of accidents or even by too long at sea, it could cloud a man's judgment and rob his hand of its cunning: in extreme, rare cases, the will broke down completely.

One deck-landing crash was not enough to do more than dent one's confidence; but there were moments, even after that one, when one could feel one's spirit curling up at the edges.

However, two days after it Butch sent me ashore for an hour's practice landings with a batsman on the aerodrome, and straight from there to the ship. "Goofers' Gallery"— that is to say the nets and every handhold on the island— was thick with spectators; but their disappointment was my relief.

XI

On December 7th 1941, the Japanese let loose their carrier-borne aircraft on Pearl Harbour, the main American naval base in the Pacific, on Oahu in the Hawaiian Islands; and three days later *Prince of Wales* and *Repulse* were sent to the bottom of the Gulf of Siam while attempting to intercept a Japanese invasion force off the Malayan coast. Did we have an uneasy feeling that but for that inexplicable error of navigation off Palisadoes we should have been there to give the two battleships the air-cover for lack of which they were sitting ducks to the Jap bombers and torpedo-aircraft?[1]

At all events, we were not there. We were 10,000 miles away drinking rum and Coca-Cola in the starlight at the Myrtle Bank Hotel, Kingston, Jamaica, and looking out on a sea that was still unrippled by the lenses of prowling periscopes.

A few days later we steamed out of Kingston for the last time, and turned south-east for Port-of-Spain, Trinidad.

[1] If we did, we were right. In Vol. III of *The Second World War*, Winston Churchill writes (p. 524): "It was decided to send as the first instalment of our Far Eastern Fleet both the *Prince of Wales* and the *Repulse*, with four destroyers, and as an essential element the modern armoured aircraft-carrier *Indomitable*. Unhappily the *Indomitable* was temporarily disabled by an accident." What might have happened if we *had* been there makes exciting guesswork.

My father, whom I had not seen since September 1939, was in Grenada, and I cabled him to join me if he could. He managed to pick up a lift in a U.S. Army bomber, and we met at Government House where we stayed at the invitation of the Governor, Sir Hubert Young. Sir Hubert's brother, Sir Mark Young, was Governor of Hong Kong; and as the news from the Far East was deteriorating with every bulletin, the atmosphere was somewhat strained.

My father was delighted to see me in uniform. He had been a regular soldier; his war had been the Boer War; and the rig that to me was a temporary but unavoidable inconvenience, to him was a matter of ardent pride and satisfaction. It was one of the subjects on which we would never agree. I admired him tremendously, but we saw war in different terms. To me, his generation had fought the Boers for their land and the Germans for their markets, and the war we were engaged in—the lineal descendant of theirs —was nothing more glorious than a chore, the final clear-up after the ignorance and incompetence of the politicians had put every other solution out of reach; nor was it mitigated by the cant they talked to cover up their own blunders. He would not have it. War for him would always be inextricably connected with some manly sport like pig-sticking, a deliciously dangerous sport for which there was a code of rules but no major, moral implication; in fact, no moral implications at all. I could envy him his certainties; but I could not persuade him that for us they did not look like certainties; they looked like the shallowest of illusions.

Twelve hours after I came ashore—I had been given thirty-six hours leave—the ship sailed, without me. This caused something of a flap; but next day she re-appeared; and I learnt when I went back on board that there had been a U-boat scare, and as Port-of-Spain was an open anchorage, she had put to sea and flown anti-submarine patrols. They found nothing; but if there was a U-boat about, it was only the first of many that were to make each island a self-contained and beleaguered fortress within the next few weeks.

That night my father flew back to Grenada, and we sailed for South Africa at twenty-six knots.

XII

We now assumed the status, and very much the routine, that we were to have for the next three months. With our three Australian destroyers, *Nizam*, *Napier* and *Nestor*, we were an independent carrier unit, racing across the oceans, attempting to plug the gaps through which the Japs were pouring westward. As the oceans themselves were hostile, each day began with Dawn Action Stations. Guns' crews closed up; fighters were brought to stand-by or to immediate readiness, and the first anti-submarine patrol was flown off.

Before first light, a flight of four Hurricanes or Fulmars was ranged and spotted right aft, with one or two Albacores armed with depth-charges in front of them on the centre line. The engines are run up by the fitters; the fighters are switched off; the Albacores' radials tick over quietly, waiting for their crews. Over an iron sea, the ship moves quietly, stealthily. Pilot, observer and air-gunner emerge from the island and climb into their aircraft. At the guns, the guns' crews test for training and elevation; the howl of the dynamos comes through loudly above the engines. The ship turns into wind, bucking a little as she crosses the swell. The night-air has a slight edge, chilling through shorts and open shirts, as the wind comes ahead, fitfully at first over the bow, then strong and steady as the revs go up and she shudders and straightens up into the wind's eye. Aft, the Albacore pilot is strapped in, has checked the cockpit, and gives a thumb up to the flight-deck officer who is waiting with his dim blue torch for the signal from Commander Flying's position up on the island. The chock-men lie at full-length by the aircraft's wheels. Overhead, the bowl of the sky has a sombre blue glaze to it, and there is a hint of light on the farthest horizon. Only a few stars still shine with their brilliance quite undimmed.

Wings signals—a blink of blue light; the flight-deck officer switches on his torch and waves away the chocks, and the chockmen double off into the nets, dragging the chocks after them by the lashings. The spot of light revolves, rises to head height and drops. The engine opens up, and the Albacore sets off at a rapid waddle and is airborne by the end of the island.

For a moment or two I stand and watch it climb away, shivering a little in the wind. There are the destroyers now, turning as we turn. The deck lifts under my feet and trembles, every joint and stanchion vibrating, as we swing back on course. The light spread gradually from the eastern horizon; the stars go out; the wind dies; and the illimitable sea catches here and there a glint of steely light.

Reluctantly I go into the island and the pilots' ready room, into the hot, thick fug, to doze on one of the bunks or read or chat desultorily to Steve or Brian until the "Secure". By then it is full day, and the level sun, striking off the polished sea, wounds one's eyes like a flame-thrower. This early sunlight has a direct violence that makes the sweat prickle under one's skin, and it is a relief to dive below into the corridors and companionways that are still cool after the night.

It is not always so uneventful. We have few scares in the empty waters of the South Atlantic, but the squadrons and the guns' crews and the fighter-direction teams and the radar operators all have to be kept up to the mark, and so we fly as often as all the limiting conditions—the ship's schedule, the wind strength and direction, the wastage rate of aircraft—allow, intercepting a covey of Albacores, wheeling down prophetically out of the sun in dummy dive-bombing attacks, or dog-fighting among ourselves high up in the clear blue air above the glittering sea.

[84]

Between the squadrons, and particularly between the two fighter-squadrons, there is considerable private rivalry. Butch works the troops like a plantation overseer, his special boast being that every evening he can turn in to Commander Flying the state of aircraft as 100 per cent Serviceable. The C.O. of the Fulmars is, by contrast, easy-going, and does not believe in sweating his fitters and riggers long into the night in order to achieve such ideal, but at that time unnecessary, figures. His name is Willy, and he lives a calm, withdrawn kind of life and hardly ever appears in the hangar; while Butch is for ever descending (on the for'ard lift) like some lively representation of the Wrath of God and bawling for the Duty Officer or the poor harassed P.O.s or some wretched worm of a parachute packer who has left undone something or other that he ought to have done.

The point of keenest rivalry, however, was not on the deck or in the hangar but in landing on. For this there was invariably an informed and critical audience of half the ship's company; and on what they saw they judged the prowess of their squadrons. Not only had the landings themselves to be good; the interval between one landing and the next had to be reduced to the minimum. Ten seconds was the goal; a twelve-second interval between aircraft was quite good. To achieve it, the aircraft had to back each other up so closely that one was just approaching the round-down as the next ahead taxied over the barrier into the park for'ard. This required careful judgment in the air, quick work by the hookmen in clearing the wire and by the flight-deck engineer in lowering the barrier as soon as the aircraft was safely arrested, recovering the wire as soon as it was cleared, and raising the barrier as soon as the aircraft was over it, and quick work by the pilot taxying up the deck. The margin of time between success and failure—and failure meant bringing on not the next aircraft but the next but one, and a delay of half-a-minute—was about two seconds. It was extremely exciting to watch; and Commander Flying, observing everything from his eyrie, controlling nothing except by the final application of his responsibility, the red Very lights fired for the last-minute wave-off, had to restrain his authority until the last split second. If the aircraft just crossing the round-down looked settled, he could take the slight extra risk that the barrier, if it were not quite up in time, would not be needed anyway. And it was, of course, far more than a theoretical exercise in squadron, and ship's, efficiency; for a carrier has to steam into wind to land-on its aircraft, and if the wind is light from astern, she may be steaming back on her tracks—and away from any ships in company—at twenty-eight knots.

While we were on our way across the South Atlantic, the Fulmars ran into a patch of bad luck. Aircraft ranged ready to fly went unserviceable; one pilot went into the barrier, and another, realising he was going to, tried to open up and go round again, too late. His hook caught the top wire of the barrier, and he was brought down with a tremendous wallop from ten feet on to the aircraft in the park. Things like that. And Butch preened himself.

So Willy had a blitz. He summoned the pilots to the squadron office and dressed them down; from time to time he was seen picking his way about the hangar with a look of fixed distaste on his thin face; and for a time his squadron officers found it more politic not to be discovered reading the magazines in the wardroom anteroom during working hours.

Things began to look up, and one morning, with a considerable flourish, eleven Fulmars were ranged for an exercise before breakfast. This was more than they had ever succeeded in having serviceable at one time before. Of the eleven, nine eventually took off, the other two retiring with high oil pressure or coolant leaks or one of the other innumerable minor ailments to which aeroplanes about to fly are subject.

So far, so good—or fairly good. The two had rather spoilt

the effect of the take-off; the land-on should be something special. Willy came on first, and roared up the deck into the park. The deck was still damp with the night's dew, and when he clapped on his brakes, somewhere about the for'ard lift, the wheels skidded and he only just slithered to a standstill in time: another six inches and he would have been over the bows.

Number Two came on and did exactly the same thing, only he did not stop in time: his wing-tip made an ugly dent in the rudder of the C.O.'s aircraft. Number Three also opened up smartly as soon as the wire was clear, and he too skidded after he had braked. His propeller chewed a piece out of No. 2's rudder. By this time the Flight Deck Officer, and Willy, were halfway down the deck, frantically waving the pilots to slow down. Quite without avail. Their breasts were filled with a determination to make this a record land-on, and they perhaps did not see, they certainly did not obey, the apoplectic gestures of their Commanding Officer. One after another they charged up the deck, braked, skidded, and smote the next ahead. Within two minutes the entire squadron was on the deck, and every aircraft was unserviceable.

Even Commander Flying, at whose instigation the original exercise had been organised, was rendered speechless by such a holocaust. Only Butch, submitting his squadron's state of aircraft that evening (S. 12. U/S. 0.), seemed in an exceptionally benign humour, and bought The Boy a drink.

Down below, out of the sun, after dawn stand-by, there is still a vestige of coolness in the air; but the cabin is frowsty, even with the fan and the blowers all going, and The Boy—it is his morning in—lying naked on the bottom bunk with a crumpled sheet across his middle, gives frowstiness its ultimate expression. I have a quick shower in the steamy bathroom aft, change into khaki shorts, a bush-jacket and sandals, and go down two decks to the wardroom for breakfast.

The long white tables are laid, and the ship's company's letters for censoring are already in the pigeon-holes. I can't face all that halting prose so early in the morning, and read a book instead. Eight o'clock: one bell and the change of watches is piped. In a minute the watch-keepers come in, looking grey and unshaven. Jock joins me. His face is already damp with sweat, and at intervals he scratches himself savagely.

"Flea? Or crabs?"

He scowls. "This flipping prickly heat—it's getting me down." Nearly everyone has it a little, the fat ones more than the thin.

"Are you flying?"

"Ay; I've the next A/S patrol. Bloody bind!" He snorts. "You're all right—one hour's dive-bombing, half an hour's aerobatics, beating up the ship. And us——! Three hours' stooging, a hundred and twenty knots, in a flipping, clapped-out old Albacore. Jesus Christ!" He's as blind as a bat, and the most consistent deck-lander in the ship. He gobbles his breakfast and disappears crossly.

Dickie comes in and taps me on the shoulder.

"You're duty-boy, you know."

"I know." I should be in the hangar at eight o'clock, although there'll be nothing to do. It's one of Butch's regulations that the squadron duty officer must hand over to his successor personally.

"Look out; the old man's in a vile temper this morning."

Dickie grins. With his saturnine gnome's face, and his gnome's shape, a big head on a short, stocky body, already sunburnt to a deep, red mahogany, he laughs off Butch's atrocious tempers. "He wandered into the hangar at ten to eight and found a lashing adrift. Yelled for me, of course— silly old bastard! It's all yours anyway."

"Thanks. I'd better nip smartly."

Let's hope nothing too frantic goes wrong.

Sometimes it does, sometimes it doesn't. Sometimes the

aircraft that are to fly happen to be the ones at the for'ard end of the hangar; more often one at least is as far aft as it can be, and the remaining eleven have to be ranged, the twelfth extricated, and eight struck down again. This is tedious for all concerned. Our Hurricanes, having to go down the lift sideways on, are mounted on little trolleys which run on rails the full length of the hangar and on to the lift. This enables them to be pushed sideways up the hangar, straight on to the lift ready to be ranged. But there are only three sets of trolleys, so each aircraft has to be manhandled on to its trolley when it's ranged, and manhandled off again when it's struck down. The distance between the wingtip of one aircraft and the fuselage of the next is about a foot; between the elevators and the hangar bulkhead three inches or less; between our spinners and the Fulmars on the other side, perhaps three feet. So there isn't much room to play about with.

Any number of things can go wrong. The rigger in the cockpit is half a second late with the brakes as the aircraft rolls back off its trolleys—and there's a tail-plane bent: a chock, keeping the wheels firm on the trolleys, slips—and there's a wing-tip buckled: or the ship rolls: or an aircraft in the range on deck goes u/s and another has to be ranged in a hurry: or one of the starter-batteries is flat: or the electrician has forgotten to sign the 700, the form on which the aircraft's crew declare that they have done their daily inspection, and the P.O. that the plane is serviceable, and which the pilot has to sign before take-off.

And all the time the ordinary maintenance of the aircraft has to go on; the thirty-hour and sixty-hour inspections; a faulty magneto checked, a leak in a hydraulic line traced; and, as soon as the aircraft are struck down after a trip, they have to be refuelled, and if necessary re-armed. Not that that is necessary these days: more's the pity.

The smallest delay, the slightest mishap, is liable to bring the Butcher roaring and ranting into the hangar, clawing at his moustache and cursing the Petty Officers, the crews and the duty boy indiscriminately. Oh, we love him dearly, the Butcher.

Sometimes something really interesting happens. One morning I am duty boy (I very often am duty boy, for one reason or another) and the aircraft are to be ranged earlier than usual, at 0430. It is black dark on deck, with a tearing wind, for it is dead ahead and we are thrashing along at twenty-six knots. The for'ard lights in the hangar are doused, for the ship is still darkened. The lift comes down, and the first Hurricane is wheeled on, on its trolleys, and sent up to the deck, where it is taken over by the handling-party. The lift comes down again and the second is wheeled on. Up lift! The warning bell rings, and the lift goes up to fill the black, windy square of sky. We go down the hangar to fetch the third cab and bring it for'ard, ready for the lift when it comes down. It's taking the devil of a time, too. "Lift!" "Hurry up with that lift!"

At last it comes down.

"What on earth have you been doing?"

The lift-driver runs across to me, his jaw sagging.

"It's gorn, sir!" he burbles.

"Gone? What do you mean, it's gone?"

"That cab, sir. It's gorn."

"Gone where?"

His eyes roll. He almost whispers: "Over the side, sir!"

"Over the side?" O my God! "You're drunk!" (An unlikely contingency at this time and place, now I come to think of it.)

"No, honest, sir, may I never live to see my wife and two kiddies. . . ."

"But how? What happened?"

What happened was easily explained, to me. The lift-driver had taken the lift up with the aircraft on it. As the lift drew level with the flight-deck, the wind caught the side of the plane and started it rolling sideways down the deck

The author during wartime.

A Seafire taking off from *Illustrious*.

"We thumped straight into a full sou'-westerly gale."

"We fly as often as possible."

"A bump as the port wheel rides over the catapult ramp."

"The nose buried itself, and the aircraft went over on to its back."

"Smoke and steam suddenly poured from *Eagle* and in seven minutes
she turned abruptly over."

"The thousand-pounders rained down in a concentrated onslaught."

"Nelson on our beam was firing with everything she had!"

"Ugly, grubby little ships lacking both speed and grace."

on its trolleys. The flight-deck party, who should have been there to handle it, had been delayed aft; the lift-driver and the aircraft's crew had been unable to hold it; and in a couple of seconds it was sidling down the deck and gathering way with every yard. Just beyond the lift's edge, the rails stopped, and the trolleys, like de-railed coaches, went veering off towards the ship's side, with the aircraft, driven by the gale, chocked on them, and in the aircraft's cockpit, one terrified fitter.

Somewhere amidships the fitter baled out—there was nothing he could do, poor fellow—the trolleys fetched up at a good pace against the coaming at the edge of the deck, stopped abruptly and catapulted the aircraft over the side into the pom-pom below.

"It's gorn, sir."

It was not so easily explained to Butch—whose aeroplane it happened to be—when he appeared an hour later, just how it came to be in the port pom-poms with one wing slewing drunkenly above the edge of the deck.

I was duty boy for a long time after that (and had to supervise the rebuilding of the aircraft, which took eighteen hours flat, into the bargain).

XIII

We crossed the Line with due ceremony—a ceremony that included being lathered with a disgusting emulsion of flour and fuel oil and then being ducked in a canvas bath of salt water rigged on the fo'c'sle—celebrated Christmas at sea (my second in succession), and arrived in Cape Town on New Year's Eve. I, curiously enough, was duty boy; and so, more curiously, was Jock. Moreover, there was work to be done. More than one Albacore had come to grief during the past two months, and it was Jock's job to unload these carcases on to the dock. It was mine, similarly, to preside over the funeral rites of our Hurricanes, including, as a measure of justice, the corpse of my own.

"There are also some new ones to collect," said Dickie Cork who was in charge of such logistics. "They're in the freighter over there." He was looking very spruce in long whites, all set for a night ashore. Jock and I looked at one another.

"It's all right for some, isn't it," he said.

I went across to the freighter. She was an odd vessel, with very high fore and after castles which were, in effect, small hangars. Into these, just before she left England, had been stowed a dozen Swordfish, bound for the Middle East. Whoever had been responsible for lashing them down had known nothing about aircraft; and when, five days out from Liverpool, the ship had run into a gale, first one, then another, had got adrift. The crew did what they could in the way of extra lashings, but it was too late. Within twenty-four hours, the twelve aircraft were unrecognisable. Their folded mainplanes had sprung off the locking points and flogged back and forth until the main bolts had bent and they had sagged to the ground. Thereafter, the struts had collapsed, and the fabric looked as if the rats had been at it. Undercarriages had spraddled and folded, tyres had burst, engines hung dejectedly out of the air-frames, resting on the buckled blades of propellers. In all the twelve, there was not one that would ever fly again.

"I hope the Hurricanes don't look like that," I remarked to the Mate. "The C.O. will be sure to blame me."

The Hurricanes, stowed in the main holds, had been lashed down correctly and emerged on their slings without a dent. We wheeled them across the dock, and hoisted them aboard.

It was 1130 before it was all done. Jock was very bitter. "Hogmanay, and they pick the one Scotsman in the squadron to stay on board, unloading bloody prangs! Just listen to them!"

From the lighted city beneath the sleeping silhouette of

Table Mountain came the sound of music and distant, but quite distinct, revelry.

"And the bar's closed," Jock added disgustedly. "But I think one of the medicos has a bottle of rum. I will not see the New Year in sober!"

He didn't.

The following evening, we went ashore together. It was the pleasant custom of the young women of Cape Town to come and park their cars outside the dock gates of an evening, and take sailors on shore-leave for sight-seeing drives round the environs of the city. Jock and I found ourselves carried off in this way; and although the excessive plainness of their faces suggested, uncharitably, that that was why they chose to put themselves in such a strong position, their distinterested hospitality was, in fact, self-evident. It was a sticky evening, all the same.

XIV

And that was all we saw of Cape Town. A day or two later we were away again, racing up the east coast of Africa to destinations and assignments that were only revealed bit by bit, through a fog of rumour and speculation. That we were in a hurry was obvious. Our day's run was rarely less than 600 miles as we pounded northwards at an unvarying twenty-six knots. Time taken to turn the ship into wind was grudged, and more often than not, when we flew, we were punched into the air off the booster, the nautical variation of the infernal machine on which Crooky and I had risked our necks by Merseyside. The Albacores kept up their constant A/S patrols, but for them, as for the fighter-boys, it was an empty, drifting life. We were becoming acclimatised to the constant heat, and were burnt as brown as walnuts. The flight-deck was like a griddle, and the wing of an aircraft that had been ranged for twenty minutes was too hot to touch. Only on deck there was usually a breeze,

and we could remind ourselves that for this basking in the
vertical sun of noonday, for the wave that unfolded its
flawless sapphire with a shower of silver arrows at each
thrust of the sheering bow, the dyspeptic rich paid fortunes
in a less topsy-turvy time.

Below decks, the ship was like an oven; but we had even
grown used to the drenching heat in the wardroom after
dark, when the scuttles were closed, and clean shorts and
shirts, put on after a tepid shower, were wringing wet before
one reached the anteroom. One grew used to drinking too
much gin before lunch, and sleeping it off stickily in the
pulsing fug of one's cabin in the afternoon, and sweating
out whatever was left in one's dehydrated system in vicious
games of deck-hockey among the arrestor wires after tea.
And then drinking too much gin again before supper. Never
would one have so much time on one's hands again, or so
little inclination to use it to any purpose.

One grew used to keeping out of Butch's way; and used
to the sight of his long figure, like that of a huge, be-
whiskered boy-scout in khaki shorts, hunched over months-
old magazines in a corner of the anteroom. He remained as
unsociable, as unpredictable, as overbearing, as much of an
enigma, as ever. He betrayed no passions but the passion
of anger, no weaknesses but the weakness of a covert vanity,
no interests but in the meticulous detail of the squadron's
activities and the ephemeral appearances of peers and
actresses in the tattered illustrated weeklies. What dreams
and illusions were brewing behind those pale, equivocating
eyes, that thatch of fur? One never knew. Not even a
glimpse of South Africa, his native land, mellowed him or
revealed a crack in the armour of his irascibility.

At Aden we flew off the Fulmar squadron and one lot of
Albacores, put their stores and equipment and ground crews
ashore, and churned on, up the Red Sea to Port Sudan.
There fifty R.A.F. Hurricanes were waiting for us, with fifty
R.A.F. pilots to fly them and a hundred R.A.F. ground-

crew to put them together, some time, some where. In between loading fuselages and mainplanes and stowing them in the hangars, Butch dragged the squadron ashore to do A.D.D.L.'s. This was a great success. The aerodrome surface was composed of a fine red dust which the slipstream of the first aircraft taking off lifted in a fine red fog in the still and burning air. Butch himself took up a position, with the bats, at some map reference in the desert which passed for the leeward boundary of the aerodrome, and, as soon as the first aircraft took off, disappeared for good in the resulting cloud of dust. Brian on his first circuit made an accurate guess at Butch's whereabouts, came in blind and nearly knocked him down; and the rest of us flew round in the gritty murk peering for him, while he, looking more biblical and boy-scoutish than ever, stamped up and down and raged and gesticulated, and finally hurled the bats at the first aircraft to pass within range. The aircraft overheated, tempers did the same; and we finally retired with sunstroke and throats like sandpaper to the comparative luxuries of the Red Sea Hotel.

Next day we were off again, thrashing south and east with our familiars, the destroyers, our destination the crumbling Imperial frontiers in the East. The wardroom was full of R.A.F. moustaches and R.A.F. slang, and the ship had been reduced from a top-line fighting carrier to a freighter, which disgruntled us. The war news was a lengthening tally of disasters.

Off Cocos and Keeling Island, under an ironfoundry sky, we picked up a fleet-oiler—the long, familiar silhouette materialising on the desolate horizon, as solitary and prodigious as a sea-serpent in those empty oceans, to lie rolling alongside for a few hours, the lascars lounging incuriously at the rail, and then to vanish mutely into the dusk—refuelled at sea, and two days later began to assemble the R.A.F. Hurricanes. The hundred R.A.F. men turned out to have worked only on Blenheims and Lysanders and did

not know one end of a Hurricane from another; the mainplanes had all got mixed up and had to be sorted out; and
the squadron ratings and officers were in the hangar, almost
without a break, for seventy-two hours, staggering round,
twelve or fifteen to a wing, juggling with them till the right
ones were found, and juggling with them again until the
bolt-holes on wing-root and mainplane could be made to
correspond and the bolts fitted. Then fillets had to be put
on, guns loaded and checked, ailerons connected up; then
fuelling, ranging, engine-testing, lashing down, and back
on to the lift for the next one with eyes blurred with sweat
and bodies raw with prickly heat.

At the same time, our squadron had to keep dawn to dusk
fighter stand-by, and our own aircraft had to be kept
serviceable in case any Japs appeared. The squadron troops
worked like demons, and on the dead-line, a hundred miles
off the Java coast, the first twenty-five were flown off, and
the next twenty-five were ready to be ranged and flown off
after them. In the meantime we kept a standing patrol over
the ship, and Brian and I were sent off on our first operational
interception with our stomachs doing somersaults and our
thumbs on the gun-button—and that was one Sunderland
flying-boat that nearly didn't get home.

The R.A.F. pilots and their Hurricanes vanished into the
blue haze, and landed at Batavia—a brave and hopeless
gesture. Within twenty-four hours every one of the aircraft
which we had so laboriously assembled had been destroyed
by strafing Jap fighters. What happened to the pilots we
never heard.

We turned and headed west for Trincomalee, Ceylon.
Before we arrived there, Singapore had fallen.

xv

When we saw the defences of Ceylon, we were not surprised. In the air, they consisted of a flight of Swordfish

from the aircraft-carrier *Hermes*, which was boiler-cleaning in South Africa, and a handful of Wildebeestes, biplanes so ancient that they had long ago disappeared from the recognition charts. Farther east, matters were almost as bad. In Singapore itself, the only single-wing fighters were Brewster Buffaloes, an evil little aeroplane which would have done the city indifferent service if they had been fit to fly, which they were not. They were still in their crates because nobody could be found who knew how to assemble them. And if the mood of Ceylon in January 1942 was anything to judge by, it was not only the equipment that was at fault. There was an indifference to the war, and a lack of understanding of how close danger lay, that were only just changed in time. When the *Hermes'* Stringbags had first begun to do A/S pastrols from Ratmalana—the aerodrome of Colombo—they had occasionally had arguments in the circuit with Cingalese businessmen of the Colombo Flying Club who were putting in their twenty minutes' solo in Puss Moths before breakfast. Finally, one of them found himself baulked as he was coming in to land and had to go round again. The following day, a letter appeared on the squadron notice board to the effect that the members of the Colombo Flying Club would appreciate it if Fleet Air Arm pilots returning from A/S patrol would *not* cut them out of the circuit. This caused a certain amount of ribald comment in the mess—as well it might.

Trincomalee is one of the world's perfect harbours, a deep, almost land-locked bay surrounded by wooded hills. At this time it was little more than an anchorage, with a jetty and a few oil storage tanks, the burrow of Fleet oilers, a naval supply ship, a destroyer or two, perhaps a couple of submarines, and ourselves. There was practically nothing to do ashore: no clubs, hotels, cinemas and what-not. The little town had a native bazaar which fairly reeked of the mysterious east, and there was the harbour to bathe and sail in; there was Sober Island in the middle of it for picnics, and there were bush-roads where one could stroll rather aimlessly, in the cool of the evening. On board there was an occasional film, shown to the officers on the quarter-deck; and of course the deck-hockey matches, fought to the death between squadron officers and ratings, and between teams from every department in the ship, played five a side with walking-sticks and a rope puck and with virtually no rules.

Butch decided abruptly to take the squadron across to Colombo for the week-end. It was a hot still morning, and the harbour at 0830 was tranquil with that motionless, burning tranquillity of early sunlight. There was no wind at all. The booster was set for maximum acceleration, and one by one we were kicked into the air and came to, six feet above the water, semi-stalled, engine at full bore, and crept away towards the green hills trying to cheat a little speed and height. We flew due west over the swampy jungle, over the elaborate temples and shrines of Anuradhapura, and low over the sea and the fishing-canoes all down the west coast to Colombo. As the twelve of us roared overhead, the wretched fishermen dived overboard, in fear for their lives.

The week-end, closely resembling a school outing under the eye of an indulgent headmaster, was something of a strain; but one or two of us managed to escape for a time to the Mount Lavinia Hotel, where the hawkers come round to the tables on the terrace above the sea with trays of moonstones and opals, and where, for an exorbitant fee, it is possible to be taken for a short sail in (or, more properly, on) an outrigger canoe smelling strongly of fish.

At the end of the outing, we flew back to China Bay—Trinco's small grass aerodrome—and for a few days augmented the Stringbags' A/S patrols up and down the coast. Then we were away again, taking off as a squadron, and rejoining the ship at a rendezvous clear of the coast. It had a special flavour, going back to the ship after a spell ashore. The relaxation of flying from an aerodrome was forfeited once again, and the slight unease of deck-landing, the slight, continuous strains of carrier-flying, and the pleasant, close comradeship of shipboard life, resumed.

Over the aerodrome, the squadron forms up and sets off across the coast. It is early yet, and the land below has the intense bright detail of morning shadow. We are in close formation, wing-tips overlapping and rising and falling over the invisible pot-holes of the air. We can see clearly in each other's cockpits a masked and helmeted figure, the image of ourselves; and on the aircraft every stud and rivet, the corner of a gun-patch, a flake of paint.

The R.T. crackles. Butch: "Boy, damn you! Close in! Close in, Boy!" A certain amount of juggling with stick and throttle to keep in tight and turn away wrath; and then, the long, steepening dive and the first glimpse of the ship, the white water curving away from her hull, her attendant destroyers in station to port and starboard. For all her lopsidedness, her proportions are so rakish, the strength of her lines so exact, each fresh sight of her from the air has the same, compelling excitement.

The squadron breaks up, the hooks go down. For a moment or two, as one pushes back the hood and lets in a blast of cool air that sends the dust in the bottom of the cockpit swirling, the pleasure of flying, the strangeness and the wonder, obliterate anxiety. This is something to have done, to have flown so easily over a great ship on a glittering sea, to have this liberty. This is our everyday, our humdrum marvel.

And as we circle her, strung out about her sky, she turns and the huge, empty deck tilts, and the white track curves and distorts; the waves thrust outward by her swinging bulk overlap in confusion along their outer edge. Other thoughts and calculations intervene. There's the C.O. starting his approach. He's too early; he'll be sent round again. There's Crooky, backing him up. Butch'll be livid if he gets on first. Yes: there he goes. Time to tighten one's circuit a little, time to put the wheels down, time for another deck-landing. My thirty-second.

XVI

The Far East was gone. Indo-China, Malaya, the Dutch East Indies, the Philippines, the Andaman Islands, Siam. The lines of defence had been broken and the fortresses cracked; nowhere was it possible to concentrate sufficient force to halt the swarming Japs. *Indom*, the warhead of a potential Eastern Fleet, was constrained, for the time being, to continue playing the ferry. We raced back to Port Sudan, collected more R.A.F. Hurricanes, assembled them as before, and flew them off, this time to Ceylon—an operation that was chiefly remarkable for the determination of one pilot, a New Zealander, who was suffering from low oil pressure, to land back on board, although his aircraft had no arrestor hook. This, with forty-five knots of wind over the deck and before the appreciative eyes of two-thirds of the ship's company, he performed very neatly; to receive a spontaneous burst of applause from the spectators, and a blistering reprimand from Commander Flying, who attributed the exploit more to a desire to show off than to lack of oil. As he pointed out, with unanswerable logic, the time it had taken to clear the deck and raise sufficient wind would have served equally well to take him ashore.

Rid of them, we paused briefly in Trinco, and then went back to Aden to collect our stranded squadrons. They were not sorry to see us, having had an even hotter and duller time than we. Up to strength once more, we returned to Ceylon to find *Formidable* had arrived with Admiral Somerville on board, *Warspite*, the four old "R" Class battleships, two cruisers and six destroyers—the framework of a new Eastern Fleet.

Our old, solitary role was over, and we were half-sorry, half-relieved. It had brought us nothing but interminable stand-by and no glimmer of contact with the enemy; and yet, in that three months of forging about the oceans, always at speed, always alone but for our spanielling destroyers, there had been something purposeful and detached, as if we carried on some secret, personal shadow-war of our own. And in those resplendent seas, peacock-blue by day and phosphorescence-lit by night, and in our rhythmic striding over them, there had been a revealed, fantastic beauty that had little or nothing to do with war. A ship at speed is beautiful, whatever its intent, and the sea it rides, and the intolerable blue sky that arches overhead; and the aircraft that you fly has a beauty that supersedes boredom and loneliness and fear. Loneliness and fear and boredom there were, but also the over-riding logic of a dream.

XVII

Now, at last, it seemed that action was upon us. We joined *Formidable* and the remainder of the fleet, and cruised up and down to the south of Ceylon at constant readiness. The ship was electric with rumour.

And nothing happened.

On April 2nd, the fleet turned south and steamed to Addu Atoll, a remote ring of coral six hundred miles from Ceylon, and within a stone's throw of the Equator. I was in the air when we approached it, and, according to the ship's navigator, crossed and recrossed the line half a dozen times while waiting to land-on, which must be a record of some sort.

It was a place that on appearances alone would give a travel-agent a rush of adjectives to the head: white coral beaches, waving palms, a cobalt sea changing to jade-green inshore, and a sun like an ultra-violet-ray lamp. The reality was rather different. The sea inside the lagoon was tepid and brackish; the white beaches were floored with chunks of coral as jagged as a kitchen-knife that cut one's

skin to ribbons and started sores it took months to heal. The
heat was inescapable, and the flies stuck to one's skin like
limpets to a rock.

Ashore, apart from some very shy Maldive Islanders who
lived in thatch huts and vanished among the coconut trees
as soon as they saw us, there were a few disconsolate
soldiers, the garrison. Jock and I went ashore to have a
look at the place, and the first of the soldiers we saw looked
at Jock, and Jock looked at him; whereupon they fell to
pommelling and swearing at each other like the oldest of
friends, which, oddly enough, they were. There was also
one raddled Australian Flying Officer who turned up on
board in bare feet and the last disintegrating shreds of a
tropical uniform, and over them a tattered oilskin and
sou'wester. He wore a scrub of yellow beard, and his bare
legs were the colour of polished oak except where scars of
wounds slashed by the coral shone in blobs and smears,
unnaturally white. He introduced himself to a somewhat
unnerved Officer of the Watch as the R.A.F. representative.
He had been sent to the atoll to select a site for a flying-boat
base, and lived in a small bivouac tent on coconuts and an
unappetising form of local mullet. But he was on board
because he hadn't had a drink for two months. As we filled
him with gin, we wondered what black he could ever have
put up so enormous as to warrant sending him to Addu
Atoll on such an assignment.

Next day we were out again, *Warspite*, *Formid*, the
cruisers and destroyers and ourselves, leaving the four
"R"s to waddle along after us. The reason for the air of
expectancy of the previous week, and for this present sortie,
we learnt by degrees. Some weeks earlier, the Admiral had
received a report that a Japanese fleet was likely to strike
into the Indian Ocean early in April; and now the force
itself had been spotted by a Catalina from Ceylon. The aircraft had only had time to give a first sighting report before
it had been shot down. The exact size and composition of

the fleet was still not properly known: only that it was there, five hundred miles to the north-east of us, steering westward, and that it contained one, or more, carriers.

That night, as we steamed north, a striking force of Albacores, armed with torpedoes, was ranged, with their crews at readiness. As dusk deepened swiftly into darkness, the ship herself seemed to tremble with a strumming nerve of anticipation. Not many people slept. The knowledge persisted past the brink of waking: a Jap carrier-force was approaching Ceylon: we were on our way to intercept. Our chance had come at last.

We were at Action Stations before dawn, hurrying up to the flight-deck almost as if the enemy might be hull-up ahead, almost as if we might be missing something. There was no news, nothing to be seen. We rushed down to breakfast in ones and twos, lifebelts and anti-flash gear near at hand, and hurried back on deck. All was still and expectant. Pilots, observers, air-gunners, with their Mae Wests un-buttoned and their helmets hanging round their necks, moved restlessly about the deck.

"For Christ's sake, let's get at the little yellow bastards," Jock said. "What are we waiting for?"

What were we waiting for? Instead of driving north-wards at full speed, we were dawdling about on the leisurely swells. We began to get edgy with impatience.

At 1030 the fighters on deck were put at instant readiness, pilots strapped in. We sat there, sweltering, fingers on the starter button, muscles aching with the effort of waiting. There were enemy aircraft on the radar screen. A W/T message had just been received from *Dorsetshire* and *Cornwall* —those dignified symbols of an obsolete Pax Britannica— "We are being attacked by enemy dive-bombers."

Then why weren't we airborne and on our way? For Christ's sake, why?

A last message from the two cruisers as they went down, and we raged and blasphemed with frustration. Commander

Flying was bombarded with the demand, and could only answer: the Admiral says no.

All day it was the same: the sour anger of enforced inaction, of a sapping impotence.

Rumours filtered through. Colombo had been bombed. Then why, and again, why, weren't we there?

For forty-eight hours longer we steamed in desultory circles, in a state of readiness that had long since become a mockery. Just our luck, we said bitterly, to belong to the fighter-squadrons that never fought. The T.B.R. boys were equally galled. The thought of an enemy fleet just over the horizon, simply waiting to be torpedoed, was too tantalising to be borne.

On April 8th we returned to Addu Atoll; and the following day the Japs attacked Trinco, and sank *Hermes* and the destroyer *Vampire* that was accompanying her. These disasters did not improve our frame of mind.

Five days later the ship was anchored in Bombay harbour —well out of harm's way.

XVIII

It was natural enough that we should be angry at seeing our first chance of action in six months go by default; it was natural that we should see it as an unintelligible decision by Admiral Somerville. It was his decision, of course; but it was not unintelligible, and it must have been a bitter one to make. While we were at Addu Atoll the first time, he learnt —as we did not—that the Japanese force consisted of five aircraft-carriers, and four fast battleships, besides cruisers and destroyers. Against this fleet we could pit only two aircraft-carriers and one fairly modern battleship, *Warspite*. They had, therefore, a superiority in sheer numbers that would almost certainly have made any battle a foregone conclusion. For the second time in six months, our Eastern Fleet might have suffered obliteration, leaving India, Ceylon and the whole Indian Ocean an open hunting-ground. In fact, at the same time as Admiral Nagumo—he of Pearl Harbour—was attacking Ceylon, a striking force of one light carrier and six cruisers was ranging the Bay of Bengal and sinking every ship in sight. But both operations were, as it turned out, flashes in the pan. Nagumo, when he retired eastwards, had failed to bring the Eastern Fleet to battle, and had suffered such rough-handling by the Hurricanes we had flown off to Colombo and China Bay, that the attack was never followed up.

It might have been otherwise; and would have been, if we had had our say. There would have been a Battle of the Indian Ocean set down in the histories of the Second World War next to the great American carrier battles of the Coral Sea and Midway. That was what the situation demanded, and what, I dare say, Admiral Somerville would have given his right hand to have been able to achieve. As it was, the Battle of the Indian Ocean was never fought. Instead there was a small and terrible butchering of one old carrier, two lightly-armoured County Class cruisers, a destroyer, and 100,000 tons of merchant shipping, while we lurked beyond the horizon and chewed our nails and followed the tracks of the dive-bombers on our radar screens. It was from the logic of our unpreparedness that this should happen; but it was none the less disheartening for that.

XIX

Before the ship entered harbour at Bombay, the squadron was flown off, and Butch took it into his head to beat up the city. We flew in over the coast at 1,500 feet, and at that height, with the cockpit hood open, I could smell the spicy, curried smell of the city borne up on the smoke of its early morning fires. And then Butch put his nose down in a long, screaming spiral. He was never noticeably thoughtful of his wing-men, but this time he excelled himself. As the squadron roared down in tight formation over the town, so he tightened up the turn, with the result that The Boy, who was on the inside, had his wing in the street and was almost fully stalled, while I, on the outside, was at full boost and doing about 320 knots. Butch, quite comfortable in the middle, was swearing indiscriminately at both of us.

Juhu Beach is a suburb of Bombay and its seaside resort, with little villas, heavily iced with stucco, among the palm trees that overlook the muddy sea. Just behind the beach was Juhu aerodrome. There, on the short runways among the sugar cane, we landed, and there, in the baking heat, we stood by to defend India from the imaginary menace of the Japanese carrier force that was now flogging back to Japan after its punishment off Ceylon. Every now and then a Blenheim with a handful of Hurricanes in its wake flew in from Karachi and the Middle East, on their way to defend the South of India and Ceylon. Of these Hurricanes about one in every nine or ten misjudged the length of the runways and went on its nose in the ditch at the end. We worked out that if the average was no better for the whole 4,000-mile trip only about twenty per cent ever reached Madras or Colombo.[1]

When we were not standing by on the aerodrome, we used to take the train into Bombay and make either for the Taj Mahal Hotel, which backed the Gateway of India and looked out over the harbour, or for the Yacht Club or the Willingdon Club, of both of which we were honorary members. Both were wonderfully luxurious and cool after the heat and dust of the aerodrome and the city streets, and provided the sharpest of the contrasts which forced themselves on us at every corner of that seething city. To step out from the gardens of the Willingdon Club at night and pick one's way over the sleeping bodies that littered every pavement and street island was to step from one world into

[1] Churchill quotes the case of *two* squadrons of medium bombers flown from the Middle East to Java, of which only *eight aircraft* reached their destination; so it may not have been so wild a guess.

another, from the standards of elegance and comfort we took for granted into a homeless, possessionless absolute of poverty too extreme to be imagined. In the bundles of breathing rags, and in the endless variety of face and colour and costume that passed among the bullock carts and the trams, the solid, Western merchant houses and the temples, there surged the tides of a continent, fascinating, utterly bewildering, utterly strange. More vividly than anywhere I had ever been, Ceylon, the West Indies, the Mediterranean, I felt an alien here.

One day I was asked to crew a boat in a sailing race by a subaltern whom I met casually at the Yacht Club. He knew nothing about sailing, or the course of the race, there was practically no wind and the harbour was solid with merchant shipping; we had no means of communication with the Indian boatman; and when we finally crossed the finishing-line, hours later, we discovered we were the only boat left in the race. However, during the afternoon, our conversation had somehow thrown up the subject of Bradford Rep, and I had asked him if he had known Barry.

"Barry Lister? Of course. You knew he'd been killed?"

"Oh no," I cried, "not Barry!"

"Poor fellow, yes. He had an air collision, somewhere in Northern Ireland, I think. Rotten luck."

Whatever interest I had had in the race evaporated. Barry was dead. I could not believe it. Whichever else of us might be killed, I had always been sure that he would survive. He had bluffed himself out of enough awkward corners in the past, he would surely be able to bluff himself out of a little thing like that. And he was dead. What a waste it seemed; and what a waste, somehow, to be still alive.

XX

A week later we were back on board, and the ship was in the Seychelles, on her way to Madagascar and Operation

Ironclad. Madagascar was in the hands of the Vichy French, and it was feared that even if no Japanese attempt to capture it was made—an attempt which would almost certainly succeed—its harbours might still be used to sustain Jap submarines in their attacks on shipping in the Mozambique Channel and the Indian Ocean. It had therefore been decided to neutralise the island, and to neutralise especially the magnificent natural harbour of Diego Suarez at its extreme northern tip.

The plan was quite straightforward. The army was to land on the west coast before dawn on May 5th, march across the isthmus and take the town from the rear. At dawn, the Albacores would attack the aerodrome, the harbour installations and any ships in the bay with bombs, and the loyalties of the inhabitants with leaflets, bravely printed in red and blue and addressed to "Français de Madagascar" on one side, and, somewhat optimistically, to "Camarades de l'Air" *au verso*. The fighters, our Hurricanes and Fulmars, and Wildcats from *Formidable*, and from *Illustrious* which had now joined us, were to patrol the area, looking out for enemy aircraft in the air or on the ground and to cover the landing-forces.

We listened to the briefing with some pleasure. After seven months of unbroken routine, and the fiasco south of Ceylon, we were delighted at the prospect of action, even if it was action, aimed, one felt, at the wrong side.

During the afternoon of the 4th, we joined up with the fleet and with the convoy, always an exciting moment; the troopships, trudging over the quiet sea from horizon to horizon, festooned with landing-craft; the mood, almost pleasurable, of expectancy and alarm.

The Wildcats had been given the landing-beaches to look after; we had the town, the harbour, and Antsirane aerodrome, paying particular attention to the last in case the fighters, which were known to be based in the south, were flown in to make mischief. The Albacores, ranged and bombed up the night before, went off in the darkness before dawn. Brian and I had the first patrol after breakfast; we took off, crossed the coast and circled steadily in open formation at 10,000 feet. Even though we expected to see nothing, the knowledge that we were flying over hostile territory—of a sort—gave our orbiting a certain zest; and we floated above the brown land like hawks.

The huge lagoon of the harbour was empty except for the sloop *D'Entrecasteaux*; and although she had been bombed earlier that morning, she appeared to be lying placidly at anchor, without steam up, though in a different position to that described in briefing. Along the coasts there was no sign of battle. The aerodrome with its tiny hangars was deserted. Or was it?

The R.T. crackled in my earphones as Brian called up the ship.

"Hullo, Cornflower (or whatever it was), Yellow Leader calling. Aircraft on aerodrome. Propose to destroy." Even in the stilted phrases of the R.T. code there was an implicit "old boy" in Brian's voice.

After a minute or two, the ship came back. "Hullo, Cornflower Yellow One. Wait. Out."

"Roger," said Brian; and in the great empty morning sky we waited.

"Hullo, Yellow One. This is Cornflower. Go ahead. Over."

The ship was ripe for blood, as we were. They had hoped, as we had, that the French might send whatever aircraft they possessed to join the battle.

"Roger," said Brian. "Line astern, Yellow Two. Going down."

I dropped back and put the stick over and forward. The world spun round us, and the airspeed indicator needle moved up steadily as we dived in a steep singing spiral on the aerodrome. Harmless-looking black puffs of smoke appeared round us; it was quite a shock to realise what they were. "Flak, old boy," said Brian over the R.T. "Pay no regard!" There was no time to worry. Already the dry, khaki-coloured countryside below us was acquiring detail; we could see the open hangar doors, and our target on the tarmac in front. We swept round, lower and lower. From somewhere to starboard a burst of tracer came bending up towards us.

"All set, Yellow Two?"

"All set."

"Roger, old boy. Don't shoot my tail off, will you?"

The wheeling landscape settled as I straightened up, and I felt the pressure on my eyeballs. Brian was 200 yards ahead, going in in a long flat dive, very fast. I saw the tracer coming up to meet him, and the smoke whip back from his wings as he opened up. It reminded me in the heat and speed and excitement to set my own guns to fire.

A few people ran out of the hangar, and on a white road along the near-side boundary someone jumped off a donkey in a fearful hurry.

Then Brian was pulling away, and the hangar and the aircraft in front of it were in the sight. I pressed the gun button, and the guns drummed in the wings, and I could see the bullets ripping into the aircraft, already beginning to burn from Brian's attack. It was intensely satisfying, and lasted, I suppose, about ten seconds.

I still had my thumb on the button when I realised that I could see straight into the hangar, and that if I spent another two seconds on my present course I should have no alternative but to fly straight through it. As the doors the other end were closed, this proposition had nothing to recommend it, and I pulled back on the stick as sharply as I dared, waiting for the high-speed stall, the helpless sinking through the unsupporting air into the hangar roof. Then I was clear and chasing after Brian.

"That looks as if it's fixed 'em," he said. "We'll do one more run for luck."

We raced round and came in again from a slightly different angle, emptying our ammunition into the burning wreckage, and then climbed away over the harbour.

"Good show, Yellow Two," Brian said. "Hullo, Cornflower. Yellow One. Exercise completed. Instructions, please."

Cornflower came back with an unmistakable note of jubilation in his normally prim voice. "Nice work, Yellow Section. Return to base and pancake."

We left the satisfactory column of smoke and flame we had lit and flew out over the coast. The ship was into wind, all ready for us, and the deck was clear—a rare welcome.

"Don't forget to put your guns to safe," Brian said as we dropped into the circuit.

"As if I should," I said, and furtively moved the catch. There were cases on record of elated pilots landing on after an operation and, as they caught a wire, spraying the unfortunate flight-deck party with the balance of their ammunition.

There was no doubt about the stir we had created. The Wildcats had been shooting down one or two Moranes over the beaches, and the ship was passionately concerned that we should not run second to *Formidable* and *Illustrious* in the matter of scalps. Our fitters and riggers clustered round as soon as we had switched off and began to go over the aeroplanes with a magnifying-glass, looking for bullet-holes, while we were whipped straight off to the Ops Room to report to Commander Flying and Commander Ops. Butch was there, too, of course, smoothing his moustache away from his mouth and positively beaming with satisfaction.

Commander Flying opened the interrogation. He was a brisk, wiry little man with black eyebrows, and he was not normally indulgent to junior officers; but now he too beamed on us.

"Nice work, Fids. One up to 880." This expressed exactly what Butch was obviously thinking, and he succeeded in looking quite coy. "Tell us all about it."

Brian described our attack, ending up characteristically: "No flak to speak of. It was a piece of cake, sir."

On the pad in front of him, Commander (O) jotted down: "Anti-aircraft defences light."

"Now, the aircraft: could you identify them, Fids?"

"Afraid not, sir," said Brian. "I'm not very hot on these Frog cabs."

The black eyebrows levelled themselves at me. "What about you?"

I had to admit that I couldn't either, and Commander Flying began to look a fraction less indulgent.

"You must have some idea—but first of all, how many were there? Half a dozen? More?"

Brian looked at him, one eyebrow raised. "Well, actually, no, sir," he drawled. "There was only one."

"Only one?" Commander Flying queried sharply, and glanced at Commander (O). "That wasn't the impression we got from your initial report." Commander (O) handed him the R.T. Log. "'Aircraft on aerodrome'—there it is."

"Well, sir?" Brian said, and with an almost imperceptible shrug disclaimed all responsibility for the ambiguities of the English language.

Commander Flying glared at the log for a second, and then handed it back. Butch clawed viciously at one frond of the moustache.

"This solitary aircraft, then," Commander Flying said. "Was it twin-engined?"

"No, it only had one engine, sir."

"A Morane, probably." He turned to Butch. "They're supposed to have quite a few of them down south. This must have been one the Wildcats missed." Butch nodded.

"I don't think it was a Morane, actually, sir," Brian said in his tiredest voice.

"Oh. Why not?"

"Well, sir, you see, this one was a biplane." The "biplane" came down Brian's nose in the most condescending manner possible, blowing away any number of grandiose illusions, and I fell into a nasty fit of choking to cover my laughter.

"I see," said Commander Flying, biting the words off like bits of celery.

"Single-engined biplane" Commander (O) noted on his pad, and neatly scored through the word "Morane".

Commander Flying turned to him again. "Have you got the cards there. They may be using obsolete stuff." He thumbed quickly through the identification silhouettes. "It burnt, you say?"

"Like a torch."

"Have a look through these, Fiddes."

Brian glanced at the little black pictures and was handing them to me when Butch, who was bristling well by now, snatched them from him.

"Actually," Brian said slowly, addressing the company at large, "I'm not sure that it was an operational job at all."

"Oh!" Commander Flying's eyebrows shot smartly up. "In that case, what do you think it was?"

"Well, I don't know, sir; but it looked to me a bit like the French equivalent of a Tiger Moth." The silence seemed to flow outwards, imposing itself even on the sundry, tireless voices of the ship. "But I thought it was better not to take any chances."

Butch flung down the silhouettes and stamped out of the room, muttering furiously. Commander (O) grinned a swift, fleeting grin and dropped his notes into the metal waste-paper basket. Commander Flying gave Brian and me one hard look.

"Quite," he said bitterly. "It would have saved a lot of time if you had said so at the beginning. All right, Fiddes."

We went out of the island into the bright windy sunlight on deck.

"Well," said Brian. "We did our best for them, didn't we? How about a gin, old boy?"

We dumped our flying-kit in the Ready Room and made our way down to the bar. "I thought old F seemed a bit huffy, all the same," he added, thoughtfully shaking three drops of bitters into his glass. "Oh well, never a dull, old boy. Cheers!"

XXI

There were other minor excitements. Steve came back from a patrol with a bullet in his engine, which seized finally as he caught a wire; and Dickie Howarth came back with a bullet in his bottom. There was blood on his parachute pack, and excitement knew no bounds. An Albacore failed to return from an A/S patrol: Jack Pike, his observer Colonel Brown (the "colonel" was a courtesy title that exactly matched his somewhat ponderous geniality) and their air-gunner; nor were search aircraft successful in seeing any trace of them; but as their area had not taken them more than a mile from the coast, no great anxiety was felt on their behalf. They had probably rowed ashore in their dinghy, and were waiting for the operation to be concluded.

Then, on the second day, we had another break from the monotony of town patrols. The *D'Entrecasteaux*, which we had seen at anchor in the harbour, had been hit by the Albacores on the first morning, and indeed driven ashore; but she was still able to cover the approaches of the town, and was making a nuisance of herself to the troops ashore. Inspired by Rear-Admiral Denis Boyd, who was flying his flag in *Indom* as Rear-Admiral Aircraft Carriers, six Hurricanes were sent in to strafe her.

As we came out of the Air Operations Room after being briefed, Steve remarked casually:

"I've always heard there's no future in beating up other people's warships"—a notion I confess that had occurred to me. But there was no holding Butch—even if we had wanted to. The semblances of death and glory appealed powerfully to his half-finished temperament.

We were boosted off and flew in low all the way, over the sea, over the low, bare hills of the northern part of the island, until the great harbour opened up in front of us, with the sloop in the shallows to the north of the town. She had steam up; and as we raced across the water, she let loose volumes of oily smoke that blew in a dense cloud towards us.

One after another we tore into her, guns blazing. The tracer showed up briefly as it went sparkling into the smoke: our tracer going in, and theirs coming out. I held it, thumb hard down and that intoxicating drumming of eight machine-guns shaking the whole aircraft, into the smoke until, a yard or two in front of me, the mast and aerials suddenly loomed up. I hauled back on the stick, and we went wheeling round for another run.

None of us was hit; and when we left her, she was burning merrily. Despite our scepticism as to the efficacy of .303 bullets against her plates, she was abandoned soon afterwards.

The army was still held up to the west of the town, and that night the destroyer *Anthony*, with great skill and daring, crept into the harbour and came alongside the quay, where she landed fifty Royal Marines. While she made her getaway under fire, they sneaked into the town and almost immediately captured the naval depot. At the same time, the army was on its way in; and by daybreak the following morning, it was all over.

We stayed outside for twenty-four hours and kept up patrols over the town and the beaches; but all was quiet; and next day we entered the harbour. We were just approaching the narrow entrance when a torpedo—fired, as it turned out, by a Vichy submarine—passed across our stern without doing any damage. The submarine was later sunk by the destroyers.

We were no sooner anchored than Butch, who regarded the *D'Entrecasteaux* as his own personal prize, organised a boat and went across to her with one or two of the squadron. Whatever was worth stripping out of her, they stripped; and they returned to the ship with booty that included everything movable out of the skipper's cabin—not forgetting all his confidential books, which he had neglected to destroy, and a signed and deeply compromising photograph of a popsy from Marseilles—and the ship's bell, which Butch installed in the hangar.

Later the sloop's Captain asked if he might go back on board to collect one or two of his personal possessions, and Rear-Admiral Boyd, who knew what Butch had been up to, accompanied him. They went below and entered the Captain's cabin in which nothing remained but the empty bunk. Boyd glanced round, and then remarked, without the glimmer of a smile:

"It seems you live pretty hard in the French Navy, Captain."

The Captain's reply is unfortunately not recorded.

The following day we were allowed ashore. The little town, which appeared to have in full measure the squalor peculiar to French colonies, was battened down; and the roads outside were littered with the bloated corpses of horses that had somehow contrived to get themselves killed in the fighting. The stench of dead horse hung everywhere in the dry air; and after a cursory reconnaissance into the deserted barracks—which had already been thoroughly looted by the army—we returned on board and confined our off-duty activities to taking one of the ship's boats away under sail. The harbour made a splendid sailing-ground, and the wind blew stiff and steady.

Not that the trip ashore had been uninstructive, offering, it might be said, a whiff of realism to the romantic and isolated exponent of flying. Removed from the everyday brutalities of the infantryman, even a dead horse or a ransacked barrack-room had a sort of novelty for us, though it left still unresolved that closest and most terrible relation of all, the relation between the killer and his victim. One could imagine the casual violence of war weaving these complex patterns in the humming air, making every minute more of these desperate relationships. Suddenly there seemed something utterly cold-blooded and in-excusable in not knowing whom your bullets should strike, like not knowing the face of the woman you kiss: a sense of loss and taint.

The feeling was sincere enough, even if the circumstances that provoked it were somewhat hypothetical; for in sober truth it was not very probable that any of us had killed anybody, or even any horses, during this particular operation, unless by the grossest mischance. It had been a very mild introduction to war, involving a certain amount of bravado and not very much danger. But it had been much more fun than stooging up and down the Indian Ocean, for instance; and we could at last say that we had been blooded.

XXII

We spent nearly ten days swinging round an anchor in Diego Suarez harbour, and then sailed for Kilindini, the naval base at Mombasa. From there, in two batches, the squadrons were sent on a week's leave.

Jock and I went to Nairobi together, and stayed there. We found friends quickly, and never felt impelled to leave it. After the ship, and the cities of the plains, it had a spring-time feeling about it that assuaged us after the months of heat. The people we met had something of the same clarity as the sunlight, a brittle, highly-strung appetite for life, a cool sensuality, without regrets.

Others, I must confess, were more enterprising. Moose, who was not normally given to exerting himself, went off on an expedition to climb Kilimanjaro. This was only a partial success, as they were out of condition and the lack of oxygen above 15,000 feet made them all sick; and they

returned worn out with their exertions. Dickie Howarth
had taken his rather undignified battle-scar to a farm in the
Highlands beyond Nairobi, from which he was returned
looking browner and more satyric than ever. John Young,
one of the Fulmar pilots, borrowed a .303 rifle and some
ammunition from the Marines and went off to do some
big-game-shooting up country from Mombasa. He was so
successful that he made himself liable for a £500 fine by
shooting a rhinoceros without a licence, and came back to
the ship hung about with stinking trophies.

In the middle of the second leave period, three gaunt,
dark figures suddenly appeared in Nairobi and were positively identified as the crew of the missing Albacore, Jack
Pike, the Colonel, and their air-gunner. They were thin
and hungry, and they had a story to tell that assured them
of as many large meals a day as they could eat. Their engine
had died on them while they were on A/S patrol, and they
had ditched no more than two or three hundred yards from
the northern coast of Madagascar. The ditching had been
perfectly successful, and with no particular anxiety or haste,
they inflated their aircraft dinghy and started to paddle to
shore. They had been paddling for some time before they
discovered that they were not getting any closer. They
paddled harder, and the shore-line slowly withdrew. They
paddled like madmen, and it made not the slightest difference. After several hours the line of the land had faded and
they were out in the open channel and drifting northwards
at a steady three or four knots. They continued to drift,
with feelings of increasing frustration and despair, all that
night, all the following day, all the next night, over an
empty sea. The hills of Madagascar had long ago disappeared astern. They had no food and no water. Then, on
the morning of the third day, they saw an island ahead and
their hopes revived. They started paddling again, and at
last succeeded in reaching it and scrambled ashore. It was
quite tiny, and completely uninhabited except for one

chicken. The only sustenance it offered was coconuts; the only hope, the remains of a native fishing-boat, which suggested it was used at certain seasons of the year. They had no means of ascertaining which season.

And so they settled down in the approved style, rigging a shelter out of the branches of coconut trees, and industriously trying to light a fire by rubbing two sticks together. In this they failed miserably; indeed they were quite bitter about it in telling the story afterwards. They made the fishing-boat serviceable somehow, and even made one attempt to get away in it; but the current was so strong, and so contrary to the way they wanted to go, they hastily—and only by extreme exertions—made back to the island. Every now and then they looked at the solitary fowl; but each time put off its despatch. It was their last resource; and they fortified their resolve by thinking how much more delicious it would be if they could cook it. If only they had had a magnifying-glass, or a cigarette-lighter, or a box of matches, or different sort of sticks. . . .

They had been on the island almost a month when a Hudson of South African Coastal Command, on a search for a Japanese submarine reported north of the Mozambique Channel, happened to pass overhead, and saw their signals. It returned later and dropped provisions to them—including matches, which sealed the fate of the chicken—and reported their presence to the nearest ship. Two days later they were picked up by a corvette which had been sent to get them. Then, for the first time, they learnt how far they had actually travelled in their rubber dinghy in three days and two nights: it was almost twice as far as they had imagined, 120 miles, instead of 60, and much farther to the eastward, for their island was one of the Aldabra group, north-east of Madagascar.

The story of their Robinson Crusoe act drew admiring audiences wherever they went in Nairobi, and women, in particular, were to be found hanging on their words.

XXIII

The Japanese attack on Ceylon in April, and continued sinkings by Jap submarines of shipping in the Mozambique Channel were enough to keep the atmosphere tense in Kilindini, and soon after we got back from leave the ship put to sea on account of some flap or other; but nothing happened, and after a week we returned to port. The aircraft were flown off to Port Reitz, the aerodrome outside Mombasa, while the ship did a boiler-clean. True to its traditions, 880 Squadron found itself keeping fighter stand-by, even in that unthreatened corner of Africa, while the Fulmars flew off down to Tanga, in Tanganyika, and enjoyed themselves.

On most days we flew for half an hour or so, to keep our hands in, and to break the monotony of sitting about on the edge of the aerodrome. I came back from one of these hops, soon after we had flown ashore, and put my wheels down preparatory to landing, to find that only one of them would lock. The other went down half-way and stuck. Pumping would not shift it, nor would the other normal remedy, violent manœuvres. So I called up base on the R.T. and asked for instructions. A careful landing on one wheel should not do more than damage one wing-tip as the wing dropped at the end of the landing-run; and this was what I proposed to do. Butch had other ideas. He called me up and told me to try and shake it down by bouncing the locked wheel on the surface of the aerodrome. It sounded all right; so once again I selected wheels down, and watched the port one lock and the starboard one stick. Then I put down half-flap, and approached the aerodrome, which was grass on a soft, sandy soil, on a straight run in at about 120 knots. In front of the control hut I could see the rest of the squadron gathered, the ambulance and the fire-tender standing by. I flew low over the grass, and then gently eased the stick forward and touched the wheel. Nothing happened, so I tried again, a little more vigorously. This time the wheel hit with rather more force; and instead of bouncing me back into the air in the same attitude, it dug into the soft soil and threw the nose of the aircraft down. At the same time showers of earth and dust were flung up through the wheel-housings into the cockpit. My goggles were up, and I was half-blinded. I felt the nose drop, and hauled back on the stick and opened the throttle. It was no good. The aircraft had lost flying-speed; the propeller dug into the ground and flew off; the nose buried itself, and, very slowly, the tail lifted, and the aircraft went over on to its back.

Helplessly I sat and felt it somersault, hesitating for a fraction of a second at the vertical, and then dropping sharply on to the tail-fin. The noise and dust subsided, and then there was only the hiss and spit of the engine, the sharp stench of loose petrol. I set about trying to get out. The hood had slammed shut on impact, and I could not move it. It was locked by the weight of the aircraft, pressing it down into the earth. As I hung there in my straps, listening to the escaping petrol fizzing on the hot cylinder block, waiting for the first jet of yellow flame, I realised there was nothing I could do about it. I was neatly trapped. As I knew I should be released quite quickly, if it didn't burn, the uncertainty over that particular point gave the situation a certain spice.

As soon as they saw what was going to happen, the squadron came dashing across the aerodrome, and I don't suppose it was more than a minute before they had lifted the tail and prised open the hood and released me. But even a minute can seem a remarkably long time.

Curiously, it was the final demise of the aircraft which I had originally crashed on deck eight months before. The tail unit and the last four feet of the fuselage of that one, which were all that survived, had been incorporated into another which was damaged in a minor air-collision between Butch and Steve in Norfolk, Virginia. In fact, the same part of the aircraft was still undamaged, except for a dent on the top of the fin; but it came with us no further. My own injuries amounted to a small bruise on my left thumb.

As far as the crash itself was concerned, I observed that Butch was unusually brusque to me for a day or two afterwards, and I understood this to imply that he took at least some of the blame for it. Taking into account the surface of the aerodrome, the obduracy with which the oleo-leg had jammed, and the comparatively small amount of damage a one-wheel landing would have caused, I don't think this unjust.

XXIV

June slipped away; and then, at the end of the first week of July, we rejoined the ship. No one had the faintest idea what we were going to do next; or if they did, they kept it to themselves. We turned south, paused briefly at Durban, and even more briefly at the Cape.

Obviously we were on our way home. So said the more optimistic, and the Commander was lost under requests for permission to "continue shaving"—to remove, i.e., the innumerable beards that had sprouted during our nine months away, the friezes of fair fur, the Players' advertisements, the fringes of black that seemed to put their owners' faces into mourning, the red whiskers that thrust straight out and the brown ones that curled like the Assyrian's.

Conflicting with this pleasant rumour, there grew slowly, but with increasing assurance, another. This one maintained that we were circling Africa in order to escort the next convoy to Malta. The more we thought about it, the more plausible it sounded. The Malta run was about the hottest in the book, hotter (in every sense) than the long-fought and disastrous convoys to Kola Inlet and Murmansk; and, apart from *Victorious*, we were the most experienced carrier afloat. If there was to be a Malta convoy, it was a reasonable deduction that we should be in on it.

In something under a month we swept round Africa from Mombasa to the Canaries; and when, at last, the skipper, Captain T. H. Troubridge, R.N. (known to the wardroom simply as "Tom", and a heroic figure as he stood beaming on the bridge, a tiny pair of binoculars balanced somewhere on his massive chest)—when the skipper announced with calm relish that the rumour was indeed a true bill, it hardly came as a surprise. It still had power to shock, nevertheless. No precise image formed in one's mind; only a visceral acknowledgement that the months of make-believe were over and that now, after nearly a year's roving commission, we were going in at last among the real enemy. The Germans, we knew, were in Sicily and Sardinia in strength; we should be operating within range of shore-based fighters; and a large fraction of the Luftwaffe would be taking considerable pains to see that the convoy did not get through. Whatever else it turned out to be, this was not going to be a mere solemn prank at the expense of the unhappy French. We needed no briefing to know that.

The evening after the skipper's announcement, we picked up the convoy of fourteen fast merchant ships, and the fleet that was to accompany them, outside the Straits of Gibraltar and well beyond sight of land. They made a formidable array as we took up our station among them. *Rodney* and *Nelson* with that lean, powerful profile; *Victorious*, *Eagle* and ourselves as fighting carriers, with *Argus* in reserve and *Furious* with a load of Spitfires to be flown off to Malta; seven cruisers and thirty-two destroyers: perhaps the most impressive show of British naval power ever assembled during the war so far. From it could be judged the importance with which Malta was regarded, and the scale of the opposition we might expect.

That afternoon before passing the Pillars of Hercules, the carriers put all their Hurricanes into the air, and we flew in formation over the ships as if to show them they would be well looked after. Then we landed-on; and, as dusk drew in, the great concourse of ships turned to the eastward.

Everyone knew what to expect, and the suspense had a stillness at the heart of it. Everyone knew what to expect; but no one knew what special demands would be made on him in the inevitable battle, what particular contingencies he was going to have to meet. The tension of those open factors, that personal anxiety, was discernible in people's eyes, in the wariness or the excessive casualness of their voices and movements. Excitement, fear, suspense, were a physical thing, tickling the skin, and danger something to be made light of. The mood on board was cheerful, resolute, and as taut as wire.

On the bridge, the skipper was in the best of humours, the substantial image of confidence. If he too was visited with qualms like the rest of us, he showed no sign of it; with his tremendous chest and profuse grey hair and invincible bonhomie, he seemed to steady the very ship herself. Whatever demands were made on him, he would meet them with the same vast Olympian calm.

For him, as for everyone else, there was nothing to do but make sure that everything was ready, and then wait.

During the night of August 9th, the convoy and its escorts entered the Mediterranean. From first light the following morning four fighters were kept at immediate readiness; engines warmed up, pilots strapped in. The day broke fine and clear; all round us the ships moved easily over the sea in a profound and tranquil dream. From time to time, Albacores took off on A/S patrol, others landed-on, and hardly disturbed the serenity. The aerials of the radar sets turned steadily through their 360 degrees, sweeping the empty skies. Submerged beneath the surface inaction, men pored over their sets, listened intently to the crackle of their headphones, peered through their binoculars in the look-out positions, with unblinking, rapt vigilance.

Sooner or later the peace would be shattered; and nerves, jumping at every pipe, at every change in course or revs, screamed out for it to happen and be done with.

All morning the ships steamed on in undisturbed calm. Then, suddenly, in the afternoon watch, two Wildcats from *Victorious* went tearing into the air. We moved nearer the island, hoping for tit-bits of news. The Tannoy crackled. It was the Commander: "*Victorious* has scrambled two fighters after a suspected shadower. That's all for the moment."

We waited, nerves prickling. That was how it would start, with a shadower picked up on the radar, lurking low down on the horizon or at a great height, and sending sighting reports back to base.

But not yet. This was not a shadower but a Vichy French flying-boat, probably about its lawful business, a routine trip from Toulon to Morocco. But Admiral Syfret was taking no chances. Without enthusiasm, it was shot into the sea. When it sighted our fighters, it would know that there was a fleet in the vicinity; its course would have taken it within sight of us; if it was left in peace, the news would be out. One day's less grace might make all the difference, to us, to the convoy, to Malta at the far end of the line, already on starvation rations and almost out of petrol for her fighters and ammunition for her guns.

That was the key. What happened to us, to the forty fighting ships deployed on this smooth sea, was unimportant so long as the little knot of merchantmen in the centre reached their destination. To ensure that, we were, if need be, expendable.

Dusk closed in. Peace had returned and continued all that night, the threatened, unreal peace of a dream. Many turned in fully dressed, sure that they would be at Action Stations before dawn. But the night was quiet.

We were on deck again at first light. The convoy was now south of Sardinia, and there was little chance that it would elude detection for more than an hour or two longer. Shadowers were certain, and the first standing fighter-patrols, four at a time, were sent up at dawn with instructions to keep R.T. silence unless, or until, something happened.

Nothing did. Steadily, in open formation, Brian and I circled the fleet as it forged steadily on its way in the slight early haze. Somewhere in the same sky, two more Hurricanes from *Eagle* were doing the same thing; waiting for the ship to break silence and send us off on a vector. There was no sound from her, and at the end of an hour and a half we landed-on again. Ten minutes later the first shadower was reported on the screen. The patrol in the air went after him, a Junkers 88 at 22,000 feet. Before they could get him, he put his nose down and made for home.

Now it was only a matter of time.

Readiness was stepped up. There were two in the air, two in their cockpits on deck; four standing by in the Ready Room; the remainder at immediate call. Later, in the early afternoon, it was my turn, with Brian, to fly again. *Furious* had started to fly off her Spitfires to Malta. There had still been no air attacks; but the fleet was under more or less permanent observation from snoopers. The dream was dissolving into the turbulence of waking.

The wind was chancy, and we were to be boosted off. I was in position on the catapult, engine running. The flight-deck engineer waggled the ailerons to draw my attention to something or other, and I looked out over the port side to see what he wanted. And, as I did so, I stared in shocked surprise beyond him to where *Eagle* was steaming level with us, half a mile away. For as I turned smoke and steam suddenly poured from her, she took on a heavy list to port, and the air shook with a series of muffled explosions.

Over the sound of the engine, I yelled: "*Eagle's* been hit!"

Listing to port, she swung outwards in a slow, agonised circle, and in seven minutes turned abruptly over. For a few seconds longer her bottom remained visible; and then the trapped air in her hull escaped, and with a last gust of steam and bubbles she vanished. All that remained was the troubled water, a spreading stain of oil, and the clustered black dots of her ship's company.

There had hardly been time to assimilate the fact that she had been hit before she had capsized and sunk; and when I took off a few minutes later, my mind was still numbed by what I had seen. It had come so completely without fore-warning. Our thoughts had been focused on the idea of air-attack; we had never dreamed that a U-boat would slip through the screen of destroyers to attack with such chilling precision. It was as if, at any moment, our own ship might stagger and lurch and list, and our aircraft go slithering down the deck into the sea.

In the air, we saw the whole fleet alter course, while the destroyers hounded back and forth, dropping depth-charges. The loss of *Eagle* had screwed up the tension by another full turn, and we flew our patrol with tingling nerves. And still the expected raids did not come.

The day wore on. At 2000 hours, Brian and I were back on standby. The sky was gaudy with the first high colours of sunset. In an hour and a half it would be dark, and readiness would be over for the day. We hung about on the flight-deck, Mae Wests on, helmets round our necks, gloves in sticky hands.

"Another forty minutes," Brian said, "and I should think we can call it a day."

The Tannoy crackled. "Scramble the Hurricanes! Scramble the Hurricanes!"

The fitters in the cockpits pressed the starter-buttons, and the four Merlins opened up with a blast of sound and a gust of blue smoke. As we scrambled up the wings, the crews hopped out the other side, fixing our straps with urgent fingers. Connect R.T.; switch on. Ten degrees of flap. Trim. Quick cockpit check. The ship was under full helm, racing up into wind—and we were off and climbing at full boost on a northerly vector to 20,000 feet, heads swivelling. Down to 12,000; alter course; climb to 20,000 again. And there they were, a big formation of 88's below us. One after another we peeled off and went down after them. They broke formation as they saw us coming, and Brian and I picked one and went after him. He turned and dived away, and we stuffed the nose down, full bore, willing our aircraft to make up on him. At extreme range we gave him a long burst; bits came off and smoke poured out of one engine, and then he vanished into the thickening twilight. We hadn't a hope of catching him and making sure; already he had led us away from the convoy; and so, cursing our lack of speed, we re-formed, joined up with Steve and Paddy, the other members of the flight, and started to climb back to base.

The sight we saw took our breath away. The light was slowly dying, and the ships were no more than a pattern on the grey steel plate of the sea; but where we had left them sailing peaceably through the sunset, now they were enclosed in a sparkling net of tracer and bursting shells, a mesh of fire. Every gun in fleet and convoy was firing, and the darkling air was laced with threads and beads of flame.

For a time we hunted round the fringes of it, hoping to catch somebody coming out; but the light was going, and we were running short of petrol. We had already been in the air for an hour, most of it with the throttle wide open. There was no sign of the 88's which had started it all; and it was not clear at first what the ships were still firing at. Then we saw the tracer coming morsing up towards us, and one or two black puffs of smoke burst uncomfortably close. We moved round the fleet, and the bursts followed us; and the truth could no longer be disregarded. They were firing at anything that flew.

We pulled away out of range, and called up the ship and asked for instructions. Stewart Morris's voice was never calmer or more sweetly reasonable than at that moment.

"Stand by, Yellow Flight. Will pancake you as soon as possible."

"If you'd stop shooting at us it would be a help," Brian said, without eliciting a reply.

We closed the convoy again, to test their mood, and provoked another hail of gunfire. We tried switching on navigation lights, which merely encouraged them to improve on their earlier efforts. Disheartened, we withdrew.

By now it was beginning to get dark, and in the gloom I lost the others. With the prospect of a night deck-landing at the end of it all, the situation was beginning to lose its attractions.

"Check fuel, Yellow Flight"; the urbanity of Stewart's voice gave one a sudden, sharp yearning to be back on the familiar deck. Worlds seemed to divide the dark cockpit and its glowing instruments from the dark Air Direction Room with its glowing screens, worlds of twilight sky and sea, as black now as well-water, and the spasmodic blurts of fire.

I tested the gauges of the three tanks, and found I had less than twenty gallons left, a bare half-hour's flying. On my own now, I throttled right back, cut the revs, went into fully weak mixture. It looked as if those eighteen gallons were going to have to last a long time.

Every now and then I approached the ships, still just visible below; and each time the guns opened up. At last, I dropped down to fifty feet, and ploughed slowly up and down between the screen and the convoy, waiting for a chance to find the ship, and hoping to find her into wind. From time to time one of the merchant ships on one side— they had thoughtfully been provided with four Bofors guns each against just such an opportunity—or the destroyers on the other side would spot me, and the red dots of their tracer would come drifting up at me. Once something bigger hit the water with a splash alongside, and I jerked away, frightened and angry. It was at about this point that my R.T. decided to pack up.

I was down to ten gallons, and began to go over in my mind the procedure for ditching, for if I wasn't shot down, and if I didn't find a deck to land on very soon, I should surely have to land in the sea. I jettisoned the hood and released my parachute harness and kept ducking the gusts of gunfire, and came, all at once, to the sudden, stabbing realisation that this might be the end of me. Up to that exact instant, flying up and down between the dark lanes of ships, I hadn't thought of it like that. Now it hit me, as blindly bruising as hatred, as confusing as a blow. I didn't know how I was going to get back aboard: now, for the first time, it seemed highly probable that I should not, and I understood the implications. I didn't wholly accept them; there was still a loop-hole or two through which the mind went bravely peering, past the dead-end of the inimical night.

Automatically I checked the tanks. Five gallons. The time had come for desperate measures unless I was going to accept without an effort my own approaching death. I flew in low over the convoy, disregarding the squalls of fire, in search of a ship to land on. It was now 2130 hours, and quite dark, and the first one I chose turned out to have a funnel amidships. I sheered off hurriedly, and just managed to make out what looked like a carrier astern of the convoy. I made for it, dropping hook, wheels and flaps on the way. It was difficult to see what she was doing: then I caught the glimmer of her wake, and began my approach. There wasn't a light showing; but I could see by the wake that she was under helm. Would she be into wind in time?

I steadied into the approach, and a pair of lighted bats materialised on her deck and began mechanically to wave me round. I checked my petrol for the last time. All the tanks were reading 0. There was a slight chance I might get down in one piece, even with the deck swinging: there was no chance of my getting round again. I continued my approach.

The batsman's signals were becoming a little feverish; but now I could just see the deck, swerving away to starboard under me. It was my last chance. I crammed the nose down, cut the throttle, and with the last bit of extra speed, tried to kick the aircraft into a turn to match the ship's. She was swinging too fast. The wheels touched, and the skid wiped off the undercarriage and the aircraft hit the deck and went slithering and screeching up towards the island on its belly. I hung on and waited. It stopped at last, just short of the island, on the centre-line—what was left of it.

For a fraction of a second I was too relieved to move. And then, out of the corner of my eye, I saw a tongue of blue flame flicker across the bottom of the cockpit, and I yanked the pin out of the straps and was over the side. An instant later the wreck went up in a haze of flame.

It seemed excessively ignorant to have to ask which ship I was in; and so I waited in the doorway into the island while the fire-crews doused the blaze, and Jumbo the crane lurched up and removed the bits.

"Did anyone see the pilot?" I heard close beside me.

"No. Did you?"

"I haven't seen him. Wasn't still in the cockpit, was he?"

"No."

"Well, either he must have made a ruddy quick getaway, or the kite must have landed-on by itself."

I didn't feel particularly like advertising myself, but I had to settle this.

"It's all right," I said diffidently. "I was the pilot."

They both looked at me.

"Crikey!" said one of them after a moment. "Nice work!"

"Are you all right?" asked the other.

"Fine," I said. "Only I could do with a drink."

"I'll bet. I'll take you down in a minute. The skipper wants to see you, though, first."

"I supposed he would," I said, and made my way up to the compass platform.

The Captain, when I reported to him, was very put out. "What do you mean by crashing your aircraft on my deck against a wave-off. Eh?"

"Very sorry, sir. No petrol." At least I knew now which ship I was in—the wrong one.

The Captain glared at me in the dim blue light. "Oh. I see. Very well."

Dismissed, I was guided down to the wardroom where, although the bar was shut, a bottle of gin had been left out by someone's thoughtful provision. I had two stiff ones, and felt better. The deck trembled under my feet as the ship altered course, and I suddenly remembered the remote urbanity of Stewart's voice, the moment when I had appreciated with such exactness that I might never feel a deck tremble under my feet again; and for a second or two I felt quite weak, the vivid past clashing with blurred present—a past that it was still difficult to realise hadn't happened after all.

The ship went to Action Stations before dawn next day. The braying of the bugle woke me and I jumped out of my bunk in sudden panic. Why hadn't I had a shake? I was late—and then, in the unfamiliar cabin, the memory of the previous night came back, sharp and detailed, and I felt lost and rather foolish. Somehow I must get back to *Indom*; and with the thought I remembered Butch and realised that for eighteen hours, less for it was only 0500 now, but for the timeless period since the pipe "Scramble the Hurricanes" had sent us tearing into the air, I had forgotten all about him. It wasn't often in the past ten months that I had been out of the shadow of that ill-temper for so long.

Now I must get back to the ship—but how would he take it?

I dressed hurriedly and went up and saw Commander Flying. Could they fly me over? Not a hope. Was there a spare aeroplane so that I could fly with the half-squadron of Hurricanes from *Victorious* herself? No again. *Vic*, like the other ships of her class, had lifts that were too small to take a Hurricane, and so all she had were half a dozen stowed on outriggers on the flight-deck. There were none to spare.

Disconsolately I went down the steel ladder, back on to the deck. I had lost my chance of flying on the one day that would be really busy. I was out of my own ship, cut off from the squadron, and consigned to the completely super-fluous role of spectator. I had, I realised as I blinked across the glittering stretch of water at *Indom*, a ferocious headache. I was depressed and disappointed—and, some cowardly little voice insisted, rather relieved.

To be glad, against all one's resolution, that one was out of the battle, however little one had willed it: that was the shameful thing; like turning over a piece of meat and laying bare the maggots that bred and squirmed beneath. I had to try Commander Flying again, and badger the Squadron Commander, to obliterate that horror; they were adamant; and all day the disgusting maggot-life wriggled under the surface of my brain until I could no longer tell what was good and what was rotten.

From dawn, twelve fighters were in the air continuously, with the remainder at readiness. The first big raid came in soon after 0900, a bombing attack by Junkers 88's. Twelve of them were destroyed, and only one or two ever reached the convoy to drop their bombs, and they did no damage. On board, there was ceaseless activity: the A/S patrols and fighters—Hurricanes, Fulmars, Wildcats—for the next standing patrol to be ranged and flown off, and, immediately afterwards, while the ship was still into wind, others to be landed-on, refuelled, re-armed, patched and serviced and ranged aft again ready for the next emergency. In the A.D.R. the screens were never clear of enemy aircraft: a group of torpedo-bombers trying to sneak in low; Heinkel 111's dropping mines ahead of the fleet; another bombing raid to be intercepted, broken up; and then, as one or two succeeded in breaking through the ring of fighters and the massive ack-ack fire, the white gouts of water erupting among the lines of ships. And each time the anxious wait as the spray cleared; and each time the same undiminished numbers, plodding on over the calm sea.

Reports, rumours, tales: the air was full of them. Brian and the remainder of Yellow Flight had landed safely back on *Indom* the previous evening. Tom Troubridge, weighing the risks, had decided that a carrier with half its fighters missing was going to be of little use on the desperate third day, and so had turned into wind, put his deck lights on, and steamed on a dead straight course for an hour at twenty-six knots, far beyond the limits of the destroyer screen, and had landed-on nine-tenths of the aircraft in the air. It had been my mischance to have found *Victorious* and not *Indom* in that last critical ten minutes when the last of my petrol was running out.

Butch had returned to the ship with his flight in the thick twilight and flown slowly up the starboard side, wheels down, looking as much like a Hurricane as was possible, and had received a short sharp burst from the starboard after pom-poms. Incensed, he had landed-on, flung out of his aircraft almost before it had come to rest, and storming across to the offending guns, grabbed the wretched Lieutenant in charge by the throat and nearly throttled him.

"You bloody useless bastard," he had roared at him, shaking him like a door-mat. "You brainless oaf! Don't you know a Hurricane when you see one!"

In the early afternoon, during a lull in the attacks, two fighters came screaming down out of the sun and swooped low over *Victorious*. We watched them. "Silly twats," someone remarked, "beating up the fleet at a time like this. Serve 'em right if somebody fired at them."

But nobody did, and fortunately the two smallish bombs they dropped bounced off the armoured flight-deck and exploded harmlessly in the sea. The only casualty was a starter-trolley which got badly bent; but there were some red faces among the guns' crews and they had to stand a good ribbing for not being able to distinguish a Reggiane from a Hurricane.

The pilots snatched meals as they could and rushed back on deck to take their places on the revolving wheel of readiness. And in the hangar the maintenance crews worked like men possessed to make the aircraft serviceable as they were struck down. They were coming on now with battle-damage to be repaired as well as the normal troubles of oil-leaks, coolant leaks, sprained oleo-legs and what-not. The hangar itself was a shambles as aircraft were ranged, struck down, stowed, refuelled and re-armed at top speed; and the hangar-deck became more and more slippery with oil.

The attacks continued with varying intensity all the afternoon. At a quarter-to-five, one of the destroyers went after an asdic contact and dropped a pattern of depth-charges. As she turned after the attack, a submarine abruptly surfaced astern of her and in the full view of the whole convoy. There was a cheer and a volley of gunfire, and the submarine's crew abandoned ship smartly.

An hour later the radar screens began to pick up the largest formations of enemy aircraft of the day, and it was apparent that the attacks were reaching their climax. Every available fighter was flown off, and reports flowed in of interceptions of squadrons of Junkers 87's and 88's and He 111's with heavy fighter protection. It was obviously an attempt to saturate the fleet's defences, and soon the ships' guns were opening up, the sky was pocked with bursting shells and smeared across with the smoke of burning aircraft, and the bombs began to fall. The raid had reached its peak when, suddenly, a squadron of twelve Stukas appeared, high in the sky over *Indom*. Fighters were after them, and a hurricane of flak went up from all sides, as one after another they peeled off at 12,000 feet and dived on to the ship. The 1,000-pounders rained down in a concentrated onslaught, and in a moment she had vanished behind a dense geyser of spray. Two, three, were hit and plunged across the sky into the sea: but *Indom* was hit too. Smoke and steam billowed up above the wall of water; and for a quarter of a minute it seemed as if she could never re-appear except as a smoking hulk. Then, slowly, as the mass of water heaved up by the near-misses subsided, she emerged, listing, on fire fore and aft, nearly stopped, but still afloat.

From every ship men watched her anxiously; isolated from the disaster, yet sharing it, impotent to help yet suffering the wound as if it were to their own ship and their own friends. For twenty minutes she dragged in a slow circle, her deck heeling and the smoke pouring from her. Then she began to right, and the smoke that seemed to issue from her lifts lost its density and thinned to a wisp; a signal lamp blinked: "Situation in hand", and she steadied on course.

Force Z, consisting of the battleships, the carriers and their escorts, had already turned away to the westward. Our job was done. Spitfires from Malta were ready to give the convoy fighter cover; and in the golden afternoon we left the fourteen merchantmen—fourteen, still, though one had been damaged in the last attack—with their escorts, forging eastwards on the last leg of their voyage, the last and worst. Our thoughts, too deep for words, went with them. By the morning, how many would still be afloat? How many would ever reach any destination but the bottom of the sea?

Half *Indom's* fighters were in the air when she was damaged, and, as they returned from patrol, had to be

landed on *Victorious*. They caused a scene of frantic confusion. The Hurricanes could not be struck down, and in
any case all spare hangar space was soon occupied by
visiting Fulmars; by the time the last aircraft had landed-
on, the park was choked with them right back to the after-
most barrier, and it was obvious that if the enemy chose to
attack again—and he well might so choose—we should not
be able to put a fighter up against him. Only a certain
number could be kept on deck if the ship was to use her
power; and so, as the crews checked them over, any that
were not fully serviceable or could not easily be made so
were pushed aft and overboard.

This was more than one or two opportunists could bear
to watch without a struggle; and as the condemned aircraft
were wheeled aft, a fitter or rigger could be seen wrestling
with the screws that held the clock on to the instrument
panel. Gradually the aircraft gathered momentum; more
frenzied became the efforts of the man in the cockpit; more
anxious the glances he threw at the deck slipping past;
until, six feet from the round-down, he would leap out and
off the wing, empty-handed, just as the aeroplane went
scraping over the rail into the ship's wake, to float for a
minute or two belly upwards and then disappear for good.

It took more than an hour to sort things out; and then
there were, at last, six Hurricanes, refuelled, re-armed, and
ranged aft ready for take off, with nothing in front of them.
Several members of 880 were now on board, Dickie Cork—
with six enemy aircraft shot down—among them, and I
heard the day's tidings. Butch was dead. The rear-gunner
of an He 111 had got him as he attacked from astern.
Ironically, he had impressed on us over and over again that
the stern-attack was fatal (to the attacker); but lack of
superior speed, not disobedience of his own instructions, had
been the cause of his death. Crooky was dead too, bounced
by a Me 109 before anyone could save him. Brian had been
shot down by the fleet's ack-ack, but had ditched successfully

and been picked up by the last destroyer in the screen. Most of the others had one or two to their credit, and the day's score was impressive.

"The first thing Butch said this morning," Dickie told me, "was: 'Where the devil's that man, Popham?'" They hadn't heard till later that I was kicking my heels in *Victorious*; the rumour was that I'd bought it. "You'd better fly now, anyway," Dickie said. After the ceaseless strains and exertions of the day he was still as cool and calm as if he had merely been doing half an hour's camera-gun exercises.

I looked at the day. The sun was already well down; within an hour it would be growing dark.

I nodded. "More night-landings?" I said as lightly as I could. The thought of approaching the deck in the dark again in the face of the fleet's assembled anti-aircraft armament chilled my blood.

Dickie grinned. "No night-landings. You'll be all right."

The aircraft was strange and lacked a hood among other things, and I watched the sun drop below the horizon with sheer cold terror on me. It only needs a raid to come in now, I thought, and it'll be the same caper all over again. I pushed the fear away: if a raid did come in, I might at least be able to redeem the horrible day's inaction, to forget that for that bitter moment in the morning I had been glad to be out of it. But this was the unkindest trick of all; and as I feared it, so I longed for a vector from the Fighter Direction Officer that would send us off to intercept in the gathering twilight.

Below us as we circled, the diminished fleet steamed tranquilly on; and somewhere over the horizon to the east, the rest of them were looking into the shadows with a more constant, a more instant terror in their bowels. With the wind roaring round me in the open cockpit, I knew how they were feeling. This was the intense, personal centre of war, the secret colloquy the mind carried on behind the muscles' reflexes; the shape and detail of it bearing down like a great weight on the spirit, a taste in the mouth like iron.

The R.T. crackled. "Right. Going down now." We began to lose height in a wide arc over the elephant-grey sea. The ship was turning into wind. The hooks went down. It was still light enough to see the detail of the deck as we flew past.

XXV

One more day of uneventful patrols, of restless picnicking in a strange ship, and then we were rounding the friendly, familiar hump of the Rock into the Bay of Algeciras. *Indom* went straight into dry-dock, for apart from the three direct hits she had received, she had been near-missed by several more bombs, and it was likely she had suffered underwater damage. From the air we had been able to gather a superficial idea of her punishment: it hardly prepared us for the savage disorder we found when we returned aboard. The main hits had been for'ard of the for'ard lift and aft of the after lift. The former had pierced the flight-deck and exploded in the mouth of the hangar, killing, or wounding with flash-burns, many of the ratings working on the aircraft. The force of the explosion raised the seventy-ton lift, which was up, two feet above flight-deck level, where it stuck jammed on its chains, like a cork half out of a bottle, and started a fire in the torpedo-store where, after a time, the torpedoes began to cook off. The latter also pierced the flight-deck, buckling the after lift, and laying waste the officers' cabin flats. A third thousand-pounder had struck the side of the ship just above the water-line where it had burst on impact, wrecked the wardroom anteroom, and killed the half-dozen officers—mostly off-duty pilots and observers of the Albacore squadrons, but including my cabin-mate, The Boy—who were there at the time.

Considering the amount of damage and the weight of bombs, casualties had been fairly light, the worst being among our own squadron maintenance crews. But the ship herself was strange to us, the run of her that was as familiar as home broken and interrupted by the jagged rents in her plates, the charred and splintered woodwork, the great, flapping tarpaulin anchored across the missing bulkheads in the anteroom. The strangeness of it all was enhanced by the faces that were missing; their death, during our absence, cut them off from us, for no ghosts could live among these draughty ruins: was enhanced also by the break in normal squadron life. Our aircraft were in *Victorious*, so even the routine of servicing was at an end; there was little or nothing for us to do; above all, Butch, the thundercloud in any sky however clear, had been unaccountably dispersed. His absence, like the sudden, nagging absence of a familiar pain, severed the last link with the past and completed the sense of unreality. To be so free to swim in the cold, pebbly sea and drink Tio Pepe and gobble shrimps at the Capitol, or climb the Rock or wander with no object through the narrow streets of the town, to savour the sheer, voluptuousness of being alive—we did them all at first with an unquiet conscience. Shouldn't we be doing A.D.D.L.'s, in borrowed aeroplanes, on the concrete wilderness of North Front?

Before the ship was patched up and ready for the voyage home, we heard the first wild rumours of the fate of the convoy. That first night after we had left them, they were attacked continuously by U-boats and E-boats until only half of the original fourteen were left afloat. At daylight these survivors were subjected to more massive air attacks, and at last only three (rumour said only one) entered Grand Harbour, Valletta, under their own steam. Two more— one of them the vital tanker *Ohio*, still afloat, but only just— were towed in next day. Five out of fourteen, but enough to keep the island alive for the next few vital months, and to fuel and arm not only the Spitfires that could blunt the

edge of Kesselring's attack, but also the Fleet Air Arm
Swordfish that ranged out night after night in search of
Rommel's supply ships. At a cost of one aircraft-carrier
sunk and one damaged, two cruisers sunk and one damaged,
and a number of destroyers sunk and damaged, the object
of Operation Pedestal had been achieved.

And then, in the last week of August, we were on our
way home. Despite the thirty-foot hole ripped out her hull
below the water-line which had been discovered in dock,
Indom was still capable of twenty-six knots, and with our
escort of destroyers we steamed in a wide circle out into
the Atlantic on the last lap of a voyage that had covered
90,000 miles and half the oceans of the world. The after
lift was still working, and such Fulmars and Albacores as
were still on board were ranged. The carpenters set to and
built a ramp up to the rostrum of the for'ard lift. And as we
steamed up the Irish Channel the aircraft were flown off.

As we entered the Mersey and the tugs came alongside to
shepherd us into the King George V Graving-Dock, the
ship's company fell in in a square round the damaged lifts,
and the Marine Band played the bold rousing tunes ordained
for ship's on entering harbour, and the damp September
wind, blowing the funnel-smoke to tatters, had a smell of
rain and autumn in it, the driving, small and half-forgotten
rain of home.

Asylum

I

A FTER only a week's leave, the squadron reassembled
at Stretton, on the Cheshire-Lancashire border near
Warrington. Moose had become C.O., and we
were to re-equip with Seafires. They had still to be found;
and for the time being we had a handful of old R.A.F.
Spitfires, delayed briefly on their way to the knacker's yard
in order to provide us with experience on type. The kernel
of the squadron was the same as it had been for a year,
except that Dickie Cork had got one of his own, and Brian
Fiddes was now Senior P. Johnnie Forrest, with a second
ring up, had a flight, and so had Dickie Howarth. I was no
longer junior boy: there were three or four new faces to
take the places at the bottom of the form which Crooky and
I had held unchallenged for so long.

The short leave, and a certain palpable sense of urgency
about our conversion to Seafires, suggested that the
Admiralty had another job for us in the near future. There
were rumours that we should be at sea again within six
weeks; but in aid of what we had no inkling. There was loose
talk of a Second Front, but one tended to discount it as
such.

The Hurricane was a good aeroplane, on land, on a deck
or in the air. The Spit was adequate on a runway, bad, as it
turned out, on a deck, but in the air one of the most exquisite
machines ever made by man. It was beautiful to look at
with that knife-fine wing-section and the two sheer ellipses
of its leading and trailing edges, and with that flowing line

from spinner to fin. And it was beautiful to fly, light and quick on the controls, without vices. It was always said that Mitchell's wife designed the lay-out of the cockpit; whether it was true or not, it was a pretty compliment, for it was as neat as a new kitchen. Against its incomparable virtues could be set its silly little undercarriage, which was quite inadequate against the rough and tumble of deck-landing, and the long, long nose which stretched away in front of the pilot and made him practically blind in the traditional, nose-up, deck-landing attitude. In so far as it had never been designed for a deck, it was unfair to charge the designer with these disadvantages: they were the outcome of a makeshift policy towards Fleet Air Arm aircraft which threw us on to the doubtful mercies of obsolescent R.A.F. machines, hastily modified, or on to the Americans. After the August Malta convoy, Admiral Syfret had reported: "It will be a happy day when the fleet is equipped with modern fighter aircraft"—a lament which held true of the Seafire I, which we were due to get, just as it did of the Sea Hurricane of which it was written and which they were replacing. The Seafire was faster than the Hurricane, but it was still not fast enough.

With the reorganisation of the squadron we all had new duties allotted to us, and I became Parachute Officer. For a start, I had every parachute in the squadron refitted to its owners measurements. This was partly normal routine; partly a talismanic gesture against an old fear. On deck, parachutes were invariably left in the aircraft—to avoid the danger of them coming adrift and getting tangled up in propellers—and if, in a flap, one didn't get one's own aircraft, the chances were that one didn't get one's own parachute either; and if, as had happened in the past, I, for instance, was landed with Brian's or Moose's, the straps fell off my shoulders; and if I had had to bale out, I should either have fallen clean out of the harness or come down hanging by my ankles. This had always seemed to me to be a way of increasing the hazards of flying unnecessarily; but without some Procrustean adjustment of the squadron pilots all to a mean height the risk at sea had been unavoidable. Ashore it was different. One took one's own 'chute to and from the aeroplane, and—since there was very little likelihood of one's having to bale out—one might as well have it fitting snugly, if only for comfort's sake. In a 'chute too big for one, one was forever pushing the straps back on to one's shoulders like a woman in a loose brassière.

We set about cramming in the flying, and in a week did nearly as many hours as we put in in a month at sea. It was no particular fun. On the borders of the Black Country, Stretton spent much of its time in that thick, smoky haze which is adequately described as smog. This miasma, the shocking exhalation of a million reeking industrial chimneys, extended on a still day as high as 6,000 feet, reducing visibility to a mile or two. In the late afternoon, with the low sun shining through it, it was like flying through a fine, dazzling gauze.

It was like this one afternoon at the end of the first week when six of us were detailed by Moose to go off on an hour's formation. Johnny was to lead; but his aircraft went u/s at the last minute, and we took off without him. He would join us as soon as it was fixed. In the meantime, Steve and Paddy and I and two of the new boys formed up and started to climb up through the murk. As Johnny's No. 2, I was leading until he appeared. Steve, two or three spans away, was on my right, Paddy on my left. We had no R.T.

We were about 5,000 feet, somewhere near the top limit of the smog, when Steve signalled to me that Johnny was on his way up to join us. In a low-wing monoplane one is completely blind downwards; but there was plenty of room for him—the whole sky—and I waited, expecting him to come up a little in front of us to allow us to form up on him.

Suddenly Steve's signals became more vehement, and I realised Johnny must be cutting things a bit fine. But his view, upwards, was completely clear, and he could see what he was doing. In any case, there is no language more ambiguous or hard to interpret than the limited hand-signals —beyond the few accepted ones—that a man makes to you from the cockpit of his aircraft forty or fifty feet away. I glanced at Steve again: he jerked his hand upwards so clearly that I pulled back a little on the stick.

As I did so there was a crash and a shudder and the aircraft fell out of my hands and flicked into a spin.

"Collision!" My mind registered it uncomprehendingly as I juggled with stick and rudder to pull her out of the spin, and pumped the throttle to try and catch the engine which had cut. After a few seconds she began to come out of it; and then the engine fired, fired again, and rose instantaneously to a shuddering howl that nearly tore it off its mountings. The rev-counter needle flicked round the clock and off it. Shaken to the soles of my boots, I cut the throttle. No propeller. That much was clear.

I took a quick look round. 4,000 feet. There was time to sort things out, anyway. The aircraft was gliding fairly comfortably, though needing a little stick to keep the starboard wing up, and losing height at 400 feet a minute. There was a jagged hole in the dragging wing, close in near the root: that and the loss of the propeller made up the total damage I was aware of. For the first time I thought about Johnny. What had he been playing at? What had happened to him? Had it somehow been my fault?—but I had never seen him. Part of my mind flew about in plain puzzlement while I looked round and tried to get my bearings. He had gone as invisibly as he had come; there was no sign of the others. I was somewhere south and east of the aerodrome, I knew; there were green fields below me, but no sign of it. No hope, then, of making a forced landing on the runway. So that meant picking one of the fields. They looked small, cut up by irregular little hills and patches of woodland: indifferent forced-landing country. And how would the aircraft behave at low speeds? At 120 knots she was stable enough; slower than that, the spoiled wing showed a tendency to drop.

I looked at the altimeter again: 1,800 feet. I'd better make up my mind pretty soon. I couldn't see a suitable field, and I didn't much fancy the idea of roaring into one at 120 knots, wheels up: I should probably turn over—and this time it might burn. . . .

I jettisoned the hood. 1,500 feet. Time to be going. I started a gentle turn. There was nothing in the neighbour-hood that the aircraft could harm. I straightened up; and with sudden, acute awareness of what I had to do, took the pin out of my straps. The slipstream caught one of them and whipped it away out of my reach. Now there was no alternative—thank God I'd had all the parachutes refitted.

Getting a bit low. We'll take no chances on not finding the rip-cord, remembering the pilot who baled out at 20,000 feet and never pulled the cord; only his fingers were in ribbons, and the webbing, where he had clawed for it through twenty thousand feet of screaming air; remember to look down if you lose it. But we'll take no chances all the same: right hand on the big square ring, roll her over to port with my left hand, trim her a bit nose heavy so that, upside down, she doesn't pull out and come chasing after me. Over, over, the air in this bit of unnatural aerobatics tearing at my helmet—and she won't go. She won't go! She wallows back on to an even keel, still flying. 1,050 feet—Christ, she's got to go. It's doing it left-handed; but I'm not letting go of the rip-cord. This time, over, she's stiff poised vertically on a wing-tip—and then I'm clear, shot clean out of the cockpit like a cork out of a champagne bottle, out into the streaming wind. The rip-cord—it's loose in my hand; with a yank the chute opens, hitting me hard in the crutch. For a few seconds I am completely disorientated, reeling and swaying about the horizonless sky; then the oscillation slows; I get my bearings. And now I'm floating, swaying, so easily over the fields and woods; and out of the corner of my eye I see the aircraft dive away upside down in a steepening arc, to blow up with a gout of smoke and flame in the middle of one of the small grass fields.

So gently, so easily, so slowly, one drifts down through the smoky afternoon, dangling from this great white blossom which, to my surprise, I find I can see simply by tilting my head back. The motion, so light and passive to every gust of breeze, seems to involve one in the natural order of things, with no more volition than a leaf blown by the wind or a thistle-ball upon a current of warm air. Serene, detached, and yet feeling remarkably conspicuous, I ghost down with the whole sky to myself.

I crane round. I cannot tell yet where I shall finish up; it is difficult to see, in any case, because I'm drifting gently backwards. For a time the significance of this doesn't strike me; perhaps because such a natural form of progress doesn't seem to demand any interference from me. Then, as the earth draws up towards me, I remember all I've read about landing by parachute: the shock is the same as jumping off a twelve-foot wall; crouch, and take the impact with legs slightly bent, as springy and relaxed as possible; twist the release-box and be ready to free the harness as soon as you touch; try and face the direction in which you are drifting. Try and face. . . . I came to with a start and began to collect the lines into my hands; but this immediately caused the wind to spill from one side of the canopy, and my downward speed increased. I let go in alarm. The ground was close beneath me now, and far from drifting gently towards it, I seemed to be dropping like a plummet. I peered hastily over my shoulder. I was heading for a little valley with a slope of rough, tussocky grass running down to a brook. And now I was falling fast towards it. I landed on my feet with a thump on the downward slope and went over backwards in a ball as the chute yanked me off my balance down the hill. I banged the release-box, and the harness fell away, and I grabbed it, and got to my feet. The parachute had collapsed, and I gathered up the harness and the lines and rolled the mass of silk into a bundle, slung the lot over my shoulder and set off along a dusty path by the stream. There was a country lane not far away; I had spotted it in those last few seconds before I landed.

Two small boys appeared out of the hedge-bottom.

"What happened, mister. Was you shot down? Ooooh, can I have a bit of silk? Go on, be a sport, mister. Give us a bit."

They tried to pull at the parachute, and I swore at them.

"Is there a road along here?" I asked them, to distract their attention. Yes, there was a road—ooh, give us a bit, mister!

I dragged along the path, feeling groggy suddenly, and dry-mouthed and slightly sick. My back was hurting—must have strained it as I rolled over. It might be miles, with the clumsy load of silk over my shoulder, and the fool kids yammering at me.

And then another voice: "Hullo, chum. All right, I see." I looked up. An R.A.F. Flight Lieutenant in battle-dress was coming along the path towards me.

"Yes, I'm all right," I said. "How on earth do you come to be here?"

"Saw you coming down, old boy. I'm an instructor with the Army Co-op show at Ringway. Dropping from Welli-bobs on a static line. Did my fiftieth jump the other day, 's'matter of fact." He looked at me shrewdly. "Your first, eh?"

"Yes," I said.

"Thought so. You were in a Spit, weren't you? Air collision?"

"Yes," I said.

"Ah-ha. How did you get out?—along the wing?"

"No," I said; "I rolled her over."

"Did you, by Jove? That's damned interesting." He gave a deprecating little laugh, and I could have hit him. "I've done fifty jumps, but never one I've had to do, if you see what I mean. You're the first bloke I've had a chance to talk to who's had to get out in a hurry."

"I wasn't in any particular hurry," I said. Damn his cold professional eyes.

"Hurt yourself at all?"

"Only my back a bit."

"That's quite common." He brushed it aside. "A thousand feet, you say? Bit on the low side for a free jump. Of course we drop from as little as three hundred . . ."

"Do you know what happened to the other chap?" I asked.

"Never saw him, I'm afraid. You must have pulled the cord pretty smartly, eh?"

There was a gate ahead, and a tilly parked beside it. "Let me give you a hand with that," he said as we reached the gate.

"Thanks," I said bitterly. My back was aching with the billowing weight of the 'chute, and I felt suddenly utterly miserable.

"Is there anywhere I can get a drink of water?" I asked as we climbed into the van.

"We'll fix you up at the station. You can ring up Stretton and tell them you're O.K."

All the way he discussed the technical aspects of parachute-jumping, questioning me closely as to my actions. At Ringway someone produced some water in a cup, and the Flight Lieutenant rang up Moose. They were sending transport for me.

It was ages coming, and I sat in the control tower, looking out at the Wellingtons among the trees and listening to a closely reasoned lecture on what I had done wrong.

At last it arrived, driven by an M.T. Wren I knew.

"What happened to Johnny?" I asked her.

"Lieutenant Forrest was killed," she said in a neutral voice.

"Oh God!" I said. "God damn everything."

II

Tradition demands that a pilot who bales out buys the man who packed the parachute a drink, and we convened that evening in the local pub; but it was a cheerless party. Johnny, equable, humorous, sound as a bell, was dead; killed in an accident which would never be adequately explained. The sun, glittering through the haze, must have dazzled him; but that was only contributory. If he was blinded, why did he not break away, instead of coming on up?

No one would ever know; though what happened was clear and tragic enough. His propeller had struck my starboard mainplane, and his forward speed had carried him on, through the arc of my own propeller which had cut through the tail of his aircraft forward of the tail-unit. It had fallen away, then, in a flat spin, without my ever having had a glimpse of him. It was found almost undamaged; and, bitterest irony of all, his safety-harness was undone and he had been killed by being thrown forward against the gunsight: otherwise he was uninjured. In all seeming, he had been knocked out, and had come to and started to escape from the cockpit when he was only a few feet off the ground. If he had stayed unconscious for a few seconds longer, slumped in his seat and tightly strapped in, who knows but that he might have got away with it. As it was, it was all waste and loss, and the shadow of it overhung my own escape.

The following day the Station M.O. looked at my back and sent me off to the E.M.S. Hospital at Winwick, the other side of Warrington, for an X-ray.

"It's probably only ricked," he said, "but it's not worth taking any chances."

Winwick was a forbidding-looking place on the side of a hill overlooking a valley full of allotments and railway-lines to the grimy bastions of Warrington. In normal times it was a lunatic asylum, and so indeed three-quarters of it was still. The remaining quarter—one wing—had been taken over by the emergency medical services as an orthopaedic hospital. The soiled red brick and the laundry chimney proclaimed its true purpose from the outside: the absence of door-knobs and lavatory chains confirmed it on the inside. Occasional glimpses of the inmates, gibbering, moping, making inflammatory speeches to themselves or merely behaving normally with an intense preoccupation, completed an effect that was both desolate and macabre.

Within these tile-faced, bedlamite walls I was duly X-rayed, and awaited the verdict. The place accorded admirably with my mood. I did not for an instant imagine that I had done more than strain my back; but Johnny's death, and the shock of the whole wretched affair, and the sponginess of one's nerves after the year at sea, all combined to smother me in a mood of the blackest depression. It was another of those enervating moments, as after the bombing at Luton or during that last, late patrol from the deck of *Victorious*, when the power of outward events, the war and its detailed terrors, seemed to swell to a huge maleficence, crowding and pressing down on one's spirit, threatening the very fibres of courage and resolve. Neither self-pity nor self-reproach nor fruitless exercises in comparative suffering —bracing contrasts between one's own misfortunes and the far worse disasters of others—was a specific to appease the soreness of spirit: it was as if one's whole being were an open wound which every circumstance could scarify.

The Sister came in with one of the doctors. He had a couple of X-ray pictures in his hand.

"Compression fracture of the fourth Lumbar," he said, holding them up to the light. "Clear as day." He turned to me. "We shall have to pop you into plaster for a bit, I'm afraid."

My heart curled up like a leaf in the fire. "Whatever for?"

"In common parlance, me lad, you've fractured your spine."

"But"—I said, gaping at him like a zany—"I'm perfectly all right. It only aches a bit. It can't be broken." Breaking one's back, like breaking one's neck or cutting one's throat, had a sort of traditional finality about it.

"Believe me, it is. You're lucky the spinal cord's not damaged."

"I see," I said at last. "That means I shan't be flying for a bit."

"You can forget all about flying for the next six months," he said cheerfully. "Sister will show you where the plaster-room is." At that moment there seemed nothing I wanted to do in the world so much as to go back to the squadron.

"Come along," said Sister, "and get undressed." And I was led off down the corridors of Bedlam to be mummified.

III

I stood, naked and shivering, in the plaster-room while Sister and the nurses went off on those prolonged, multi-farious jobs that always seem to crop up in a hospital the moment a patient has shed the last, darned shred of warmth and modesty. Then they drifted back and set about me. I was draped in a long, closely fitting vest and then suspended between a couple of tables with my back bent backwards like a bow and wrapped from throat to crutch in cold, wet plaster bandages. Then they wheeled me away to bed to dry off.

This was really the last indignity. To have walked in under my own steam, and then, on the flimsiest of pretexts, to be swaddled down in these clammy cement cerements— for six months!—it was too much. I glanced cautiously round at the occupants of the other beds. They were mostly rather older than I, all soldiers to judge by the khaki uniforms about: chaps with complicated and terrible wounds incurred in tanks in the Western Desert in mortal combat with the Afrika Korps, no doubt. I would keep pretty quiet, I decided, about my "broken back" among such undoubted heroes.

After a day or two I discovered I was in good company. One member of the ward had in fact been in tanks in the desert, a mordant and attractive character with an energetic mind, by the name of John Moseley. He was equally reticent about his wound and his rank; but I discovered after a time that he had a leg badly smashed by a bullet, and that he was a Lieutenant only because he had been wounded two days before his Acting Captaincy was due to become substantive, and thus, according to the oddly ruthless regulations of the army, had dropped from the rank of Acting Major, which he held when he was shot up, to his confirmed rank, which was still Lieutenant. He was the only battle casualty. The rest, mostly elderly Captains, had got themselves stomach ulcers on lonely gunsights, or fallen off their motor-bicycles and knocked their shins about. The ulcers lived on a melancholy diet of milk and boiled cod; the motor-cyclists clumped about in great plaster boots, such as I had worn at Luton, and discussed technically and at length the symptoms and progress of their maladies. Far from being the giants I had imagined them, they were the wastage on the edges of war, the human equivalent of the damaged training-aircraft, the crashed army-trucks, and all the other miscellaneous equipment broken or written off by misfortune or carelessness or ineptitude, a sorry, dust-bin crew. Among such gash, I had all the status of a teapot without a spout.

As a hospital, it had its compensations. Its staff was civilian and mostly Irish; its regulations were few and lax; and it was about a quarter of a mile from a pub which never ran out of whisky. Once my plaster jacket had hardened, I was allowed up, and found I could just manage to squeeze a uniform over it. The effect was curious, and to the casual passer-by, rather baffling. There was obviously something unusual about this erect and portly figure—but what? They were more baffled still when, as invariably happened if I was out with a woman, she dropped her handbag and sent the contents rolling all over the road; for I either had to let her scrabble for her own possessions—which excited critical comment along the lines of "Call yourself an officer and a gentleman!"—or lower myself precariously to my knees, the only method I had of reaching the ground— which invited ribaldry. I don't remember taking a girl out without being faced with this dilemma at least once during the course of the evening. Much of our time was spent, inevitably, at the pub; and we must have been a grisly-looking crew, the stalkers, the limpers, the hobblers, the crutch-ridden, the chair-borne, scrambling up the road to the Swan at opening-time, like some unsavoury rout out of a Rowlandson print.

From time to time our numbers were increased. An A.T.A. pilot was brought in, after a crash in a Hurricane on take-off, with a broken back and all the grim complications of paraplegia. Every ten days or so, he would be wheeled away to be worked on by the surgeons; and at the end of three months he was taking a few shaky steps. After Christmas another Fleet Air Arm type turned up, a

New Zealand Observer who had fallen down a cellar on Christmas Eve and damaged his leg—no comment; and a Naval Warrant Officer from a neighbouring Air Mechanic Training Station, with some elusive complaint or other.

He at once set to work on me to come and lecture to them. "They've never seen a carrier and you have; it's just what they need."

Never having given a lecture in my life, I refused with some vehemence; but he was as persistent as an insurance-salesman and at last, taking my "Oh well, I'll think about it" as an affirmative, was cured and vanished. I thought no more about it; but a week later he rang me up.

"Tomorrow evening. O.K.?"

"What for?"

"Your talk. It's all fixed. I'll pick you up about six; we'll have a few gins and an early supper; you can give your lecture; and then we'll retire to the wardroom and have some beer. O.K.?" He had me cornered, and he knew it. Oh well, I thought as I gave him a grudging assent, a couple of dozen blokes in a class-room were nothing to be afraid of; and hastily scribbled a few ideas down on the back of a postcard.

We had the few gins and went for a stroll round the camp. After a time we reached the gymnasium, one of those over-grown Nissen huts, the size of a hangar, given over to badminton and E.N.S.A.

"Now," said the W.O., "how would you like the lighting?"

"Lighting?" I said. "What's it for?" I thought he was asking my advice for the stage management of some impending concert-party.

"Your lecture?"

"*What?*" I said; and then: "How many people are there going to be—there?"—pointing weakly at the rows of chairs that were finally lost to sight in the dust-haze several hundred yards away.

"Only about five hundred to-night," he said, as cool as you please.

I gulped. "Light it how you like; as long as you leave me in deep shadow. And, for God's sake," I added on a sudden twinge of inspiration, "a blackboard. And lots of chalk."

When we returned to the hall after bolting a particularly indigestible supper, the rows and rows of chairs were full of sailors who obviously thought they had been going to have a film-show, and would much rather have been playing rummy in the wet canteen anyway. The last, unwilling Christian, I was led into the arena; the little noose of introductory euphemism was unknotted, and I was left to the lions.

For a good ten seconds my mind remained in a state of rigid coma. I stood on the platform and goggled and boggled at them, and felt the palms of my hands oozing. Then, somehow, I managed to burble out some blithering opening sentence and got my eyes to focus on the crumpled little postcard, and remembered what I was going to say, and said it. I went on saying it for an hour and ten minutes, when the Captain, who was in the front row, sent his messenger up on to the stage with orders to stop me, by force if necessary. I was sweating profusely by this time, and thoroughly enjoying myself; and if I had not been down to my last inch of chalk—all the rest lay broken and scattered round me, and I wasn't going down on all fours for anyone—force might have been necessary. As it was I submitted; attempted to answer a barrage of fatuous questions and nearly started a free fight in the back rows by setting one questioner against another, and was released at last for the promised beer. Through the ensuing fog of alcohol and cigarette smoke, I realised that I hadn't enjoyed anything so much for a long time.

[157]

IV

The months passed slowly. Early on, my original jacket was cut away and I was re-interred in an even less fashionable attitude. Apart from the itching, which was almost intolerable, and the grooves the weight of the plaster cut into my hips, and the inconvenience of not being able to bend, it was not much of a penance, physically speaking. The penance was the enforced idleness; the hospital routine which was irking to people who were perfectly well apart from some local injury; and the fretful habit of mind that tends to prosper among people whose only common interest lies in their bodily afflictions.

The purpose of the squadron's hurried changeover to Seafires became apparent when, on November 8th, Operation Torch—the Allied landings in North Africa—was announced. 880 had embarked in the old carrier *Argus*, and had provided part of the fighter-cover for the tremendous convoys that had converged on Oran and Algiers. On the whole they had had a fairly dull time, for as in all the actions of the French between 1940 and 1944, the same tragic and disabling equivocation persisted.

Jock was posted to a Barracuda squadron nearby, and brought the double advantages of his boozy companionship, and also news of many of our old friends. It was a sad recital, for most of them were dead. Robin had been killed in an accident; Michael had been shot down attacking shipping at night in the Med in a Stringbag; Mandy had been killed dog-fighting with an Me 109 in a Fulmar. Ronnie Martin was dead. Of the rest, those who still survived were scattered about the world, in carriers or on aerodromes in the Desert, in East Africa and Ceylon.

Already, it was as if I had ceased to belong to their company. My flying-pay had come to an end; and if the relaxed, relaxing life in a hospital ward was a world as

[158]

enclosed as that in a fighter squadron, they had nothing in common.

But, at last, it came to an end. After four months of constant itching and a mediaeval squalor next to my skin, I was cut out of my mould, and walked away, two feet above the ground, to lie in the deepest, hottest bath since Cleopatra slid naked into her asses' milk. It was the most exquisite, most abandoned, most luxurious, most voluptuous sensation it is possible to imagine. My back was as stiff as a rod; but the sheer absence of weight was like an alleviation of gravity, and I floated about the world feeling as light as a balloon and as clean as a knife.

Freed from my carapace, I was delivered into the hands of a strapping young woman by the name of Miss Rowbotham who daily for a month pounded and pummelled my back with all the controlled force of her twelve or thirteen stone. She felt she had failed in her job if, by the time she had finished with you, you could not get your elbows on the ground without bending your knees. I got a bad pass from her, finally; threw a party for the staff at which nine gallons of beer were drunk in the first hour and a half, and was despatched with an awesome hangover to Lee-on-Solent for medical boarding.

There the learned doctors, disguised as Commanders and Captains R.N., could find nothing wrong with my back, but something very wrong with my eyes; and for a fortnight I attended a sort of clinic, run by two amiable Wrens, and peered madly into a thing like a stereoscope until I could practically see round corners.

Lee, the headquarters of the Fleet Air Arm, was a sort of lost dogs' home where innumerable disconsolate Sub.-Lts. (A) R.N.V.R. mooched round waiting for medical boards, courses in this or that, postings, courts martial and other solemn ceremonies. It had permanent buildings, unlike almost every other Naval Air Station, and more than its share of Commanders and above; the discipline was strict and impersonal in a way almost unknown at sea in wartime; and the standard duty of the lost dogs was to spend untold hours per day sitting in a small, brick office on the edge of the aerodrome, checking aircraft in and out. This so depressed one character—a puckish ex-Albacore pilot from *Indom*—that he borrowed a revolver and blew his brains out. There were moments when it seemed like a pretty good idea at that.

At least it seemed almost beyond doubt that I should go back to first-line flying; so I put off following his example, and at the end of March 1943—six and a half months after the collision—I was posted to a refresher course with 748 Squadron at St. Merryn in North Cornwall.

v

Cornwall in the spring, flying again, and a squadron so well-organised that on four days out of seven one's flying for the day was done by lunch-time, and there were the lengthening afternoons in which to explore the coast and the countryside on borrowed bicycles or on foot: after hospital and Lee, it was a refresher course indeed.

How the spring had the power to pierce the heart then, insisting so blatantly that life continued however diligently man might go about his futile business of destruction. The very anguish of the contrast had a heady, dangerous action on one's mind, and every nerve was a cat's whisker, twitching alike at pain and pleasure. One was free of responsibilities; life held a threat of brevity; and the moment had a compound intensity for which experience could provide no context, no reference. And if it appeared that war was an evil whose only remedy was peace, whose only relief was these rare moments lived just beyond its reach, it appeared equally that the rare moments were all the more precious for being so precarious. All emotions were heightened, and the range of possible emotions, their pitch and tension, was correspondingly increased. And as one yearned for peace one knew in one's more sanguine moments that peace would never be like this.

The stolen month slipped away with its routine practices, formation, attacks, dogfights, ground-strafing, air-firing; and when, before the buds in the high hedges were fully opened, I was posted to the Orkneys once more, to join a Seafire squadron, I left behind me in Cornwall the girl who would one day be my wife.

Sea-time—H.M.S. *Illustrious, Campania,* and *Striker*

Sea-time—H.M.S. *Illustrious, Campania* and *Striker*

I

894 Squadron, when I joined it at the end of April 1943, was engaged with a number of others, Seafires and Grumman Wildcats, in wing exercises. This was something new for the Fleet Air Arm which had so far only been able to muster a number of carriers to work in company for special occasions and by special effort, with no opportunities for the squadrons involved to work up together. Now here were four or five squadrons all buzzing about in the variable cloud over the Orkneys at the same time, some providing fighter-cover, high, middle and low, others carrying out low-level attacks on the aerodrome, while the R.A.F. from Wick came screaming down out of the sun in the role of enemy formations, and all under the eye of a wing leader, Buster Hallett. This would have been fun if I had not had, as I soon discovered, a lively terror of air-collision. I only really enjoyed flying in conditions of extreme visibility with no other aircraft in the sky. For such tender apprehensions, this was shock treatment; and on more than one occasion the squadron popped out of cloud to meet a squadron of Wildcats, at the same height but on the opposite course, just about to pop in; a situation that was resolved rather after the manner of a man interlocking his fingers. But here, of course, where all the circumstances favoured collisions en masse, and a runaway imagination had no difficulty in picturing clots of aeroplanes, inextricably

tangled up and descending earthwards after the fashion of the dogfights to the death of World War One, no one ever ran into anyone else. As this was against all the laws of probability, my first week or two were somewhat uneasy.

What these balbos were in aid of was clear enough in conception, but not in their particular application. It was evident that at some period in the reasonably close future the Admiralty envisaged a task force of British aircraft-carriers operating together in the same way as the Americans were operating in the Pacific; but where and when were a matter of speculation.

We spent a couple of months at Hatston on this caper before being bundled down to *Argus* for some deck-landings. As the pilot in the squadron with the greatest number to my name, I distinguished myself by missing all the wires on my first two approaches. Fortunately the barrier was not in use and I opened up and went round again with nothing damaged except my pride.

894 was the complete reverse of 880 in the age and experience of its pilots. The C.O., Dick Turnbull, a straight-ring two-and-a-half, had been on fighter course at Yeovilton with me as a very scruffy Sub, and this was his first squadron. Norman Lester, our Senior Pilot, and Peter Weston, the leader of the other flight, were both also of about the same vintage; and this tended to make the C.O. a little wary with us. It is difficult to wield convincing authority over your contemporaries and erstwhile drinking-companions, even when you have two and a half stripes to their one.

Norman, a slight chap with the face of a Walt Disney wolf and thinning fair hair, had been on one of the courses I had dallied with at Luton; Peter and I had been at St. Vincent together. He was one of those small, mild, inconspicuous people who surprise one by suddenly disclosing highly formed and firmly held opinions on abstruse subjects, quite at variance with their manner and appearance. His were for small-boat sailing and designing, and the novels of Thackeray; twin loves about which he was normally reticent, but which, if sufficiently provoked, he would defend with vehemence.

A third old friend was Nobby Clarke, who had been at Kingston; and a new one, Harry Palmer, a tall, bearded South African (another one!) with the vagueness and courtesy of manner of an elderly peer, and a working sense of humour.

We were the old men of the squadron. The others were, in flying terms, of a later generation, and had mostly been trained in the States. They, with the New Zealanders who were filling the squadrons in increasing numbers, were the new, expanding Fleet Air Arm, just as we had been to the early courses who had done their flying training in 1939 or 1940, and as they, the R.N.V.R. proper, had been to the R.N. (A) pilots and observers of pre-war days. But there was an even bigger difference now, the difference of vastly increased numbers. In two years, the Branch had already ceased to be the compact, intimate service of the early part of the war.

Immediately after doing our deck-landings in *Argus* we moved from the Orkneys to Macrihanish and the Clyde where *Illustrious*, for which we were bound, was re-equipping after her return from the Indian Ocean. We joined her finally in July.

Once again we found ourselves at the mercy of the haphazardness of the Fleet Air Arm's development, for the Seafire, like the Hurricane before it, had fixed wings of too great a span to go down the lifts; and so we were consigned to outriggers, of which there were three only, and a permanent deck-park. This arrangement had the abstract disadvantage of making us feel as if we didn't quite belong, and the more concrete one of always being in someone's way. We were like the late-arrived guests who are dossed down on the drawing-room sofa or the billiard-table or in the bath and after a time begin to acquire a harassed and slightly persecuted look. There were practical disadvantages as well: the difficulty of maintenance in the open air, and of perpetual handling of aircraft up and down the deck. These would have been quite acceptable if they had not coincided with our first experience of the Seafire's special faults as a deck-landing aircraft. Minor damage was frequent, for apparently faultless landings often buckled an oleo-leg or bent a propeller tip: major prangs were not unknown: and what with one thing and another, Commander Flying quickly acquired a strong aversion to using us if he could possibly use the Wildcats. And so we struggled to keep the aeroplanes serviceable, or to make them so, subject to the recurring necessity of pushing them up and down the deck, and watched the Wildcats, of which there were two squadrons on board, come bouncing in from absurd heights with complete impunity. It was all a little disheartening; and there seemed no immediate prospect of our redeeming ourselves in the sceptical eyes of Commander Flying.

The two T.B.R. squadrons were equipped with Barracudas: it was our first glimpse of this extraordinary aeroplane at close quarters. It was of immense size and of truly formidable aspect, for the solution of each problem with which the designers had been faced had generated fresh problems involving fresh and increasingly elaborate solutions. Thus it had a high wing in order to give the observer and air-gunner maximum downward visibility. But to produce an undercarriage that would retract into it meant a vast structure which looked as if it had been built out of components robbed from the Forth Bridge. And in order to enable the flight-deck party to handle the wings for folding —they were out of reach of the tallest—special handles had to be provided, with tackles to give a proper purchase. The same massive clumsiness obtained in the design of the dive-brakes and the high-set tailplane with its supporting struts; and, as if to complete the resemblance to an umbrella blown inside-out, the mainplanes were decorated with numbers of highly complicated aerials. But worst of all, the Barracuda had idiosyncrasies which were never sorted out; and soon after we joined *Illustrious* I heard with bitter sorrow that Jock, flying one straight and level at 1,500 feet, had for no accountable reason got out of control and gone straight in. For all his wild ways, he was an impeccable pilot, and this accident was difficult to explain. Nor was his an isolated case.

To complete one's sense of disgust at this freak it was only necessary to look at its American equivalent, the Grumman Avenger, with its businesslike barrel body, with wings that could be spread and folded automatically by the pilot in the cockpit, and with a notable superiority both in performance and load.

The conclusions one came to, looking at the Seafire that was too big for the lifts and too delicate for deck-work, and the Barracuda, that monument of misapplied ingenuity, were plain enough: the Fleet Air Arm was paying a stiff price for its twenty years of servitude to the R.A.F. Not without justice did Admiral Cunningham describe that experiment as "a ghastly failure".

II

We completed our work-up and joined the Home Fleet in Scapa for a short spell. It was while we were there that a Skua pilot, towing a drogue for the benefit of the fleet's anti-aircraft armament, and observing that the bursts were appearing at the correct height but slightly ahead of his aircraft, sent a signal to the ships concerned: "Would like to remind you I am pulling this thing, not pushing it!"

Nothing of note occurred, and by the beginning of August we were back in the Clyde. Among the ships, familiar and unfamiliar, at anchor round us at the Tail of the Bank was one at least that was unmistakable—the *Queen Mary*. She was busy taking on her last-minute complement of troops and stores; and that evening she sailed. She, and the *Queen Elizabeth*, were already famous for their continuous solitary journeys, without escort and at high speed, over the oceans; and we watched her slip away into the dusk with admiration. What a target for a U-boat, or a Focke Wulfe Condor roaming wide over the Atlantic!

That night we slipped down the Clyde after her, and the rumour got round that we were to escort her clear of the danger area because Churchill was on board. And so it proved; though we were able to provide precious little escort, for we steamed round the north of Ireland at thirty knots and ran head-on into a full sou'westerly gale. In driving rain and spray next morning we flew off a couple of Wildcats—the Seafires pleaded to be allowed to fly, in vain—and they disappeared into the scudding cloud to the south. Half an hour later the weather worsened again, and they were recalled. They landed-on without mishap over the bucking round-down, and all aircraft were struck down— except the unfortunate Seafires which we parked in the lee of the island, where they had to ride it out under storm-lashings.

The *Queen Mary* was not far away, but in the dirty weather we never had a glimpse of her. I wish we had, as the Wildcat pilots described her, battering into the big seas and with the heavy spray sweeping over her from bow to stern at masthead height. Our destroyers were frequently invisible for seconds at a time, to reappear with green water sluicing off them as they burst through the waves; and soon they flashed that they could not maintain the tremendous pace, and would heave-to and pick us up on our return.

Illustrious herself was taking about all she could stand. With nothing else to do I made my way up to the Admiral's Bridge above the Compass Platform—a wonderful position, for there was no Admiral on board and it was deserted, perched high above the flight-deck—and for hours on end stood peering out through the streaming armoured glass, fascinated by the pitch and yaw of the huge empty deck as the bows smashed into the oncoming waves and scooped up tons of water, white and green, that went swirling down the deck, flawed and harried this way and that by the gusting of the wind until they were lifted and swept away aft in fine curtains of spray.

We kept it up for thirty-six hours, crashing on into the gale, and ready to fly off if there were cause; but there was none; and once beyond the reach of the land we turned back to pick up our destroyers, and left the *Queen Mary* to her own devices. By the time we were back in the Clyde, the papers were carrying the news that Churchill was confabulating with Roosevelt in Quebec.

III

We stayed in the Clyde for a week and worked over, not for the first time, the sparse diversions of those two dour towns, Greenock and Gourock. The Bay Hotel at the latter was the best of them, if one could afford the taxi-fare to get there, and it was the scene of several memorable parties. One was so memorable that the manager intervened, picked on our flight-deck officer, a genial, carefree Lieutenant R.N.R. who happened to be hanging from the chandelier, and forbade him ever to darken the doors of the hotel again. Next evening an incredibly sinister figure in a coarse black beard and smoked spectacles, dressed in civilian clothes, arrived at the Bay and spent a pleasant and fairly roistering night of it in the bar. At closing time, when the manager appeared, this unsavoury-looking individual strolled up to him, removed whiskers and specs with a flourish and wished him a very cordial good night. Thereafter the ban was removed.

As usual, our next destination was a matter of guesswork, swayed by every breeze of rumour; but when we sailed, we turned south out of the uncertain summer of the Irish Sea towards the bland sunlight of Gibraltar. There we found Rear-Admiral Vian's force of escort carriers, *Battler*, *Attacker*, *Hunter* and *Stalker*, with the light-fleet maintenance-carrier *Unicorn* acting in the same role, furiously exercising together in Algeciras Bay.

This, it seemed, had been one of the purposes in view when we were working as a wing at Hatston; but what operation were we to cover? The invasion of Sicily, launched on July 9th, had just been successfully completed. The next step would seem to be landings on the mainland of Italy; and there was a certain amount of excitement at the prospect, for Jerry was known to be there in force still, and he would presumably resist any attempt at invasion in his usual thorough fashion. But it was only guesswork.

We stayed for a day or two in Gib, and then steamed through the Western Mediterranean to Malta. As we stood by on deck or flew, with the aid of our somewhat temperamental long-range tanks, two-hour umbrella patrols over the ship, it seemed incredible that this was the same sea as that over which, almost exactly a year ago, the August Malta convoy had fought its way. Now, though the ship was alert, the skies were clear and no aircraft, German or Italian, opposed our passage, and we reached Valletta without incident.

For *Illustrious* herself, the passage through the narrows south of Sicily and the entry into Grand Harbour were a triumphant restatement of British naval power in the Mediterranean. For it was in these waters, on January 10th 1941, no more than two months after her brilliant attack on the Italian battle fleet in Taranto Harbour, that she had been ferociously handled by dive-bombers and with her lifts out of action, her flight-deck holed and her steering-gear disabled, had limped into Malta, to lie alongside for twelve days under continuous attack from the air.

It had taken two and a half years to reassert the dominance which Admiral Cunningham had achieved immediately before that first, drastic entry of the Luftwaffe; and it was fitting that *Illustrious* should be there to witness and affirm it. She entered Grand Harbour on this occasion with the ship's company manning the flight-deck, the marine band playing, and the white ensign fluttering bravely from the jackstaff.

We had flown off some of our aircraft to Takali, and put in a certain amount of practice-flying while the ship was in port. On the way to the aerodrome, and on trips ashore, we saw all we needed of the work of two and a half years' concentrated bombing attack. Much of Valletta had been pounded to rubble, from which the yellow dust blew off in clouds in the hot, dry sunlight. Such shops as remained were empty; rations were still short; and the life of the city, so recently redeemed from the nightmare borders of starvation and high explosive, had a drawn and makeshift air. Nevertheless, as each place has its own peculiar flavour which it retains beyond damage and disintegration, so Valletta, even with its steep and narrow stairways choked with ruined masonry, kept still its antique, fortress air. In the high and holy city of Rabat, above the central plain, the feeling was stronger still, for its strait streets within their wall had been spared destruction—a destruction which might have impressed even those artists at such work, the Crusaders.

But our impressions were fleeting, and our concerns more with the serviceability of aircraft than the activities of the Knights of St. John; and at the beginning of September we flew on board once more. The ship was in company with *Formidable*, *Nelson*, *Rodney*, *Warspite* and *Valiant*, and a number of cruisers and destroyers, and as we steamed west and north through the Sicilian Channel, we were briefed in the plan of Operation Avalanche.

The United States Fifth Army and the British Tenth Corps were to land on the Italian mainland in the Gulf of

Salerno. They would be operating here beyond the reach of shore-based fighters, and so cover would be provided by Seafires from the four Woolworth carriers and *Unicorn*, which were to be known as Force V. In order that they should be able to use all their aircraft over the landing-beaches without the necessity of providing protection for their own force, fighter umbrellas over Force V would be sustained by the Wildcats and Seafires of Force H, which would also be on the look-out for any attempted interference with the invasion forces by the Italian fleet.

On the evening of the 8th we were all tensed up for the following day when the news came through on the wardroom radio that Italy had surrendered and the Italian fleet was already on its way to Malta under escort. The immediate reaction to this dramatic news was, of course, that we might as well all go home; and the wardroom buzzed with sudden speculation. Then the Skipper, Captain Cunliffe, spoke to the ship's company over the Tannoy, reassuring them that the operation would proceed as planned. He had barely finished when Action Stations was sounded and the fleet was attacked by a squadron of Junkers 88's. It was pitch dark by this time, and when the guns opened up we went out on to the quarter-deck to watch it. *Nelson* on our beam was firing with everything she had, including her sixteen-inch: as the big guns flashed, the ship's superstructure was briefly and brilliantly lit up, isolated in the surrounding blackness. Then, as one's eyes recovered from the glare, one could see the streams of sparks pouring up into the sky; then again the blinding flash and the deafening roar, until one's jaws ached with the noise.

The action lasted half-an-hour; three or four of the attacking aircraft had been shot down and the rest had drawn off without inflicting any damage on our ships. We steamed on through the night to our appointed position off the coast; but we turned in with our minds curiously confused.

[174]

IV

We were up at first light next morning, and with the Wildcats kept a fighter umbrella over both Force V and Force H throughout the hours of daylight. After the alarms of the previous evening we were at first inspired with the healthiest expectations of having something to shoot at and were sharply alert; but as patrol succeeded patrol with hardly a rumour of enemy aircraft to break the monotony of cruising round in the thick blue haze we slowly came to the realisation that Jerry was not going to play. It was the culminating anti-climax, the final bathos. The Wildcats did shoot down one shadower, but even he had first of all been reported as a "big bogey", a mistake which fitted snugly into the general pattern of things and provoked Michael Hordern, our fighter-direction officer, to a neat impromptu quotation:

"Thou wretched, rash, intruding fool, farewell!
    I took thee for thy better."

There were alarms from time to time, and I spent one or two patrols with my No. 2 harrying about in the curiously opaque light looking for reputed bogeys, but without success. This haze, which was constant throughout the operation, made our routine flights even duller than they would have been, for it reduced visibility to a mile or two, and from fifteen or twenty thousand feet we could see no glimmer of the land, and precious little of the ships directly below us. We might have been a couple of goldfish drifting round in a bowl of thick blue glass for all the reference we appeared to have to the battles rumoured to be raging on that remote shore.

The absence of enemy aircraft was disappointing to our particular squadron for a special reason over and above the general ones of frustration and ennui, for we were the guinea-pigs for a new piece of equipment so secret and so immodest that I hesitate to introduce it into this narrative. It consisted, in effect, of a special flying-suit, skin-tight, double-skinned and contrived of a remarkably obscene type of pale blue, pimply rubber. Into these rubber combinations we were squeezed and laced like Scarlett O'Hara into her corsets; they were then filled up, like a hotwater bottle, through a nozzle situated well up on one's chest. This operation, conducted after one was seated in the aircraft by the fitter or rigger, produced the most curious sensation, a sort of liquid tickle against one's skin slightly reminiscent of the disasters of one's early youth during a long day at the seaside or a long tea-party in a strange house.

You may well inquire, as we did when we first saw them, the purpose of these odd garments. It was this. One of the limiting factors in air-combat is the fact that the force acting on a pilot when he is pulling out of a dive or doing a very tight turn is a multiplication of the force of gravity which tends to drag the blood away from his head, with the result that he blacks out. This force is known as G; and the normally healthy pilot blacks out when the force acting on him increases to 2 or 3G. Blacking out itself is momentary, and has no after effects: as soon as the turn is relaxed or the pull-out eased, as soon, in fact, as G is reduced to the tolerable maximum, one comes to, with one's senses unimpaired. But in dog-fighting, where victory may depend on tightening up the turn as far as possible, and where much of one's time is spent on the grey fringes of black-out, a pilot who is equipped to stand an extra load of G and still remain conscious is obviously at a tremendous advantage. To achieve this—to raise a pilot's G threshold—our pale blue combinations were intended. As the value of G was raised, so the water in the suit was forced down and exerted such pressure on one's abdomen that one's blood remained to a great extent where it was, and one's threshold was raised to 4 or 5G.

They were given to us to try because there was little

likelihood of our being shot down over enemy territory:
had the powers-that-be but known it, no secret can ever
have been so safe. As a corollary, of course, we had no
opportunity of testing them in combat. But in dog-fights
among ourselves, between one pilot dressed and one undressed, we had no doubts about their efficacy. The only
doubts we had were about their comfort when standing by
on deck, since a suit of closely-fitting rubber underclothes
is not the thing one would normally choose to wear while
waiting to fly in a temperature of eighty or thereabouts.

v

It was only gradually, and then in the main through
B.B.C. news broadcasts from London, that we learnt that
all was not going as well as was hoped ashore. The Germans,
warned by the armistice, had manned all the defences themselves before the expedition landed, and resisted with such
purpose that on D plus three, when Monte Corvino airfield
was supposed to be in operation it was still under shell-fire,
and the following day the port of Salerno itself was recap-
tured and there was a lively danger of the invading armies
being flung back into the sea.

Warships were despatched post-haste to North Africa to
bring up reinforcements; a landing-strip was improvised
at Paestum and twenty Seafires from the escort carriers,
and six of ours, were flown ashore to provide immediate
air-cover. Dick Turnbull took our six ashore, where they
operated for four or five days under artillery fire among the
olive and citrus groves and, owing to Jerry's habit of only
carrying out snap raids first thing in the morning or last
thing at night, had a dull and rather beastly time. I, with
the remainder of the squadron, was despatched to *Unicorn*
to augment her depleted fighter-strength. Depleted it
certainly was. The twenty aircraft which the Woolworths
had sent ashore represented all that remained serviceable,

out of a hundred or more, after the first three days of the operation. This was in part due to the complete lack of wind. The small carriers were only capable of a maximum speed of seventeen or eighteen knots, and this, with no natural wind to supplement it, was on the low side for deck-landing. In conjunction with a lack of experience on the part of many of the pilots, it resulted in accidents of truly astonishing number and complexity. They had come roaring in, shedding their hooks, thumping into the barrier, dropping into the park, going over the side, until the hangars were choked with wrecks. We, with our bigger decks and higher speed, had no such troubles: in fact the squadron got through the operation without a prang at all, which somewhat mitigated the unfortunate impression which Commander Flying had formed of us.

We spent two more days operating from *Unicorn*, and then the ship withdrew to join the escorts at Bizerta, and we flew back to Malta to join *Illustrious*. By this time the rest of the squadron had also arrived, having flown overland from Paestum; and *Valiant* and *Warspite* had closed the coast and joined the battle as extra artillery. Jerry had had no answer to the colossal pounding of their fifteen-inch guns—though *Warspite* was later damaged by a novel radio-controlled bomb—and the situation was quickly restored.

To us all these goings-on ashore had remained completely unreal throughout. While we floated peacefully about in the haze that had an almost purple tinge low down and completely masked the land, busy with our thoughts and false alarms, men were cowering under bombardment among the dusty trees or fighting it out with bayonets and revolvers. The two functions were irreconcilable, and we seemed to be in the safe and privileged position of spectators when we did not feel detached from the action altogether.

By the end of September we were back in Gib. We stayed for a week, and then sailed for U.K. Twelve hours out we were ordered back to Gib again, for a further ten, idle days.

There was a rumour that we were standing by for an operation against the Azores: in fact, on October 10th, Portugal at last agreed to let the allies set up bases there, and we were presumably at readiness in case of a strong German reaction. There was none; and by the middle of October we were back in the Clyde.

VI

One insignificant, but to me oddly important, thing happened the night before we left Gibraltar finally. Peter Weston, Nobby and I had had a run ashore and were returning through the dockyard rather late and in good spirits. We were fooling about, and as a result of a friendly brawl with Pete, I tripped and went headlong down a flight of wooden steps. (I always maintained that he pushed me; he denied it categorically; but that is neither here nor there.) I landed on my left knee and the third finger of my right hand, spraining the former and ripping the nail off the latter. As injuries they weren't anything dramatic. But the knee stiffened up so much that I was off flying during the five days of the voyage home, and spent most of the time lying in my bunk with my leg stretched straight out in front of me. With nothing else to do, I started work on a long poem, which had been fermenting for some time, based on life in a carrier. I wrote hard all the way home, the lines flowed easily; and when we went on leave after arriving back in England, there was little left to be done to it but to type it out.

John Lane's had already got a whole parcel of poems of mine which they had liked well enough not to send back in the enclosed stamped addressed envelope; and C. J. Greenwood, one of their directors, had advised me to submit them officially for a competition which the firm was then running, and which was open until January 1944. As soon as "Against the Lightning" was finished, I sent it off to him and asked him to submit it with the others.

During the ensuing three months I went through the refined torture reserved for authors whose first books remain under prolonged adjudication; but at last the results were announced with my still-untitled "Poems" as the winner in the poetry section. I heard subsequently that the long poem, the occasion for the writing of which had been provided by the brawl in Gibraltar dockyard, had tipped the scales in my favour.

Shortly after the announcement of the awards, the Admiralty P.R.O.'s got hold of me, took my photograph, and concocted a really deplorable piece of journalese out of it all which appeared in the evening papers under the headline: FLEET PILOT WITH BROKEN BACK WRITES £150 POEM or, in another version: HE WROTE POEMS IN HOSPITAL AFTER AIR CRASH.

With a cool disregard for the truth, they had substituted the collision with Johnny for the affair in Gib, and as the source of inspiration, not simply as the source of opportunity; and, with an equally cool disregard for my pleading, and commonsense, they sent the story out six months before the book was published. For mishandling such excellent free publicity, C.J. always—a little unfairly—blamed me; but in fact by the time the story appeared I was at sea again, with even less control over the fantasies of the Admiralty Press Department.

One rather touching piece of fan-mail followed. An old lady in Leeds was so affected by the story that she sent me an ancient copy of Shakespeare's Histories and a pack of playing cards, thereby disclosing a nice sense of balance in the matter of how best one should employ one's leisure time.

VII

We spent the balance of the year at Henstridge in the valley of the Blackwater in Somerset. We re-equipped with new aircraft, Seafire III's, and spent our days chasing up and down Salisbury Plain making camera-gun attacks on the mixed bag of aeroplanes that was always in the air above it. Our new aircraft were a considerable improvement on the old; and on an oxygen climb and height test one morning at the end of December, Mattholi and I succeeded in reaching 38,000 feet—10,000 feet higher than I, certainly, had ever been before. It was a brilliantly cold, clear, pale and lonely world we found up there, and our aircraft left white coils of vapour behind them as they yawed and staggered in the bright thin air.

Dora, whom I had left at St. Merryn, was now at Chivenor, near Barnstaple; and apart from spending our leave together, we contrived to meet from time to time, and came to know the obscure branch lines that link South Somerset and North Devon through a patient familiarity with their meanderings.

Then in January we left the cosy, well-known and well-loved West Country and moved north to Burscough, a wretched, sodden aerodrome on the flat, black lands behind Blackpool. A move north usually meant that we were preparing for sea again; but we had only been there a fortnight when, to my intense disgust, a signal came through to say that I had been selected for a batting course, and directing me to proceed on leave until further notice.

The job of Deck Landing Control Officer—to give him his full title—or "batsman", the officer responsible for bringing the aircraft down on to the deck, was coming to be regarded by the Admiralty as one of increasing importance. This was not because of any change in the nature of the job itself, but because of the reluctance of any sane person to do it if he could possibly arrange to do anything else. Although the batsman's signals were orders which the pilot was obliged to obey, and every carrier had its own batsman, there had been no standard procedure by which batsmen were appointed or trained. Normally they were pilots who were off flying for one reason or another, and had been co-opted into doing it; and for this reason, and because it was an unenviable job, it was regarded with a mixture of dislike and disdain by pilots who were fit for first-line flying. The dislike and the disdain persisted; but now, under the energetic partisanship of Commander Everett, an energetic little man who tended to overrate the importance of his particular pet, the science of batting was being launched with all the paraphernalia of a training-school at Easthaven in Angus, and an unhappy collection of second-line pilots condemned to doing interminable A.D.D.L.'s. There, trained D.L.C.O.'s were turned out with the multiple blessing of Everett himself and of Lieutenant Commander Arthur Darley, his number two, who had been our batsman in *Illustrious* and whose signals I had sedulously disregarded for the four months we were on board, on their heads. For all their attempts to make batting respectable, however, they were unable to find enough suckers to volunteer for the job, and had to rely on arbitrary selection from squadrons. This was how I had been picked; and very cross I was about it, too. I was enjoying flying again after the shaky-dos of 1942; I had done thirty landings in Seafires without breaking anything; and, above all, though I did not mind deck-landing myelf, I had an almost superstitious dislike of watching other people do it. Not for me the forefront of "Goofers' Gallery" where the spectators, like the spectators of other nerve-racking sports, stood tensely awaiting the next display of virtuosity, the next prang.

Now, like some sort of ringmaster, I should have to watch every landing, and carry a high theoretical responsibility for the accidents while receiving no credit for the others.

However, my grouses went unheard. From this summons, at this time, there was no appeal, for the fleet, with the number of its carriers increasing month by month, was short of batsmen; the call for volunteers had fallen on ears most resolutely deaf, and if you didn't like it you could lump it.

VIII

A fortnight later I found myself standing at the end of a runway on the windy coast of Angus, waving a pair of outsize yellow ping-pong bats at a succession of passing Stringbags. In between I spent much time supplicating Everett and Arthur Darley in turn to release me and send me back to a squadron—without avail. Thereafter the course spent ten days in *Argus*, batting aircraft on to a deck; a period memorable mainly for a long and sparkling walk over the hills of Bute with all the Clyde spread out at one's feet in the brief, golden afternoon; and a sail in *Argus's* fourteen-foot dinghy one blowy day in Lamlash harbour. The dinghy was normally stowed just under the funnel vents aft, and was as black as a coalie's gig. We got away all right; then the port shrouds parted, nearly carrying away the mast and putting us on a lee-shore. We got them re-rigged, and were working ourselves an offing when the starboard ones parted, and we drifted back where we had started from. The comments of the Officer of the Watch, who had been watching us through his telescope, were acid; and so, as we scrambled back on board covered from head to foot in soot, were ours.

And then the course was over, and we received our blessing and departed once more on leave, pending appointment. I employed my time well by collecting my £150 from John Lane's, and getting married.

Less than a week later I was standing among the puddles on the grey steel deck of *Campania*, one of the new British escort-carriers, then commissioning in Belfast. She was not bad-looking, of her kind, though I distrusted at once the narrowness of the flight-deck and the poverty of arrester-wires, of which there were only five. There were, as yet, no aircraft, and only the rudiments of a flight-deck party, and the Admiralty's zeal to get me there seemed a little mis-placed—a fact that the Captain tacitly admitted by letting me go off and finish my honeymoon.

I rejoined the ship in the Clyde a few days later, and for the next six weeks we were hard at it. If it had simply been a matter of training up the flight-deck party and its Petty Officers—none of whom had ever seen or handled an aircraft in their lives—or of ranging, flying off and landing-on our squadron of Swordfish and the six Wildcats, or merely of shaking down a new ship's company in a new ship, there would probably have been nothing remarkable about our working-up period. Indeed, about these routine matters there was little that was remarkable unless it was that the harmony between the various departments, and particularly between the Air Department and the Executive —essential equally for an efficient and a happy ship—seemed singularly absent. The prime cause of this was the Commander, a cruiser man who seemed unable to accept the fact that aircraft and their crews cannot conveniently keep ship's routine but must fly when they are required, and the Commander Flying who was willing to placate him. Between these two I was a lost soul, neither a watch-keeping ship's officer nor a member of the squadron, though I was still on flying pay; and while I naturally regarded myself as part of the Air Department, the Commander claimed me as a ship's officer. It was not long before we clashed.

Above this ground-swell of uncertainty and unrest, we had more precise troubles in the shape of three Fulmars equipped for night-fighting. This was an experiment, and, for Arctic convoys during the winter, a necessary one. It was just unfortunate, from the point of view of the pilots, and myself, that the carrier with the narrowest deck and the fewest wires should have been chosen for it. For the pilots, a landing eight or ten feet off the centre-line meant putting a wheel in the nets; for me it meant a hasty dive into my safety-net; and while off-centre landings are not uncommon during the day, they are rather more common in all

[184]

the confusing and variable factors of darkness. The climax to a series of mishaps came when Flossie Howell, the most senior of the three, and the most experienced, rejected my signals to get up a bit and hitting the round-down, was bounced back into the air in a shower of sparks and landed with an impressive screeching of torn metal at my feet, while I was busy making up my mind which way to run.

These incidents, for which I took my share of the blame —how deservedly I could not say, but the uncertainty was utterly depressing and did not increase anybody's confidence, least of all my own—combined with the mood of the ship, gave our working-up period a nagging, nightmarish quality which far exceeded my worst anticipations of a batsman's life.

However, at last, with the question of the practicability of operating Fulmars at night still open, we were deemed operational, and proceeded to sea to join our first convoy. This proved to be a four-and-a-half knotter, which we escorted to within a hundred miles of Gib, where we picked up another four-and-a-half knotter which we escorted back to the Clyde. We did three of these running, thirty days at sea each, rolling over the summer swells in conditions of glazed windlessness, and never, in three long months, sighting a U-boat or a hostile aircraft. A/S patrols were ranged, flew off, and were brought back on over the swaggering stern, dawn, noonday and dusk, with trance-like monotony; and while we were engaged on these funerary occasions, millions of men were swarming ashore at Arromanches, a few hundred miles to the eastward, and continents were rocking.

At the end of the third of these double journeys we returned to the Clyde, and aircrew were sent on leave. I applied to the Commander to go with them, and was refused. I was newly-married; my wife was in Glasgow: perhaps the temptation would have been too much even if I had not known—as perhaps he did not—that in other carriers the wretched batsman got the same leave as aircrew automatically.

Very angry, I slipped ashore, and we had a glorious week-end at Luss, on the shores of Loch Lomond—glorious except, perhaps, for the slight shadow that lay over it of what would happen when I returned aboard, for I am not a comfortable law-breaker, and not all my righteous indignation sufficed to silence a fretting conscience.

I strolled back on board on Monday morning, to be politely informed by the Commander's messenger that I was under open arrest. In a way it was something of a relief; and apart from making me feel slightly self-conscious, it appeared to involve no other noticeable inconvenience. Later that morning he sent for me.

We were very frank with each other, and for the first time, now that he had me at such a complete disadvantage that we were able to meet, as it were, on equal terms, I realised that I liked him, and that, in fact, he probably liked me.

After I had said my piece, he glanced at me and then rubbed his hand over his jutting nose and chin, promontories that made up a cartoonist's profile of a Commander R.N. After a bit he said:

"I think perhaps you'd better repeat to the Captain what you've just said to me."

I said I should be delighted; and we climbed up topsides to the Skipper's cabin in the little sawn-off island, and went over it all again. The Skipper listened thoughtfully, and I could not begin to guess what he was thinking. He had none of the Commander's frank and ruddy geniality; it was a face which, with its controlled severity, belonged more to a country parson, or the headmaster of a minor public school. If he had turned to Commander Flying, who was standing, fidgeting, with an expression of pained detachment on his face, and asked him to pass the cane, I should not have been surprised by any incongruity. When, on my last Sunday at school, I had been caught reading Dorothy Sayers during the headmaster's divinity class, there had been a scene of similarly portentous triviality.

"What you're saying in effect," the Skipper said when I had finished, "is that you don't like the ship, and you imagine that the ship doesn't like you. Right?"

I took a deep breath and said: "Right, sir." I hadn't put it quite as frankly as all that.

"Well, you won't get out of being a batsman by such behaviour." I denied hotly that I had had any such thought; though I should have been glad enough if it had led to that.

We haggled over the question for a minute or two; and then he made one or two remarks that were somewhat to the point, and packed me off.

Forty-eight hours later I was transferred to *Striker*, which was anchored half a mile away across the Clyde, and *Striker's* batsman took my place in *Campania*. I was greeted with: "Bad luck, chum: this is the ship that puts in more sea-time than all the rest of the Woolworths put together."

It eased my guilt-complex a bit to discover that far from recoiling at the prospect, I was quite looking forward to it.

IX

Striker was one of the escort carriers—known aptly as Woolworths—being turned out at great speed and in prodigious numbers by American shipyards. Ugly, grubby little ships, lacking both speed and grace, they had been built in a hurry for a specific purpose at a time when it seemed that only constant air-protection could reduce the fearful slaughter of merchant ships in convoy by U-boats. If they lacked the solid, cared-for elegance of the fleet-carriers, this was not simply because of the extreme functionalism of their fitting and design—though no amount of spit and polish could ever have made them beautiful: it was also because they did, in fact, spend so much time at sea.

In this they were more nearly related to the battered, salt-bitten frigates and corvettes whose presence with every convoy was taken for granted after 1943; and although they might turn up from time to time, as at Salerno, in the more glamorous rôle of a striking force, their lack of speed alone was sufficient to keep them apart from the main fleet. Having been bred to big carriers, I could deplore the Woolworths' squat lines and humdrum tasks, and appreciate how hard they worked.

I joined at noon, and at 1500 was batting-on the aircraft, which had been ashore at Macrihanish, as we steamed down the Clyde. After *Campania*'s narrow iron deck, everything was strange. *Striker*'s was broad in comparison, and being a little shorter, looked broader than it actually was, and it was planked, after the American style, and cut across, every six or eight feet, with scuppers covered with fretted metal gratings which acted as cleats for lashing down aircraft. There were ten arrester wires, which looked like sound practice after *Campania*'s five.

As the ship turned into wind and the hot fume from the funnel vents eddied across the deck and I took my place on the unfamiliar platform while the aircraft buzzed round waiting to come on, I had a moment or two of misgiving. The move from one ship to the other had been so sudden I had had little time for anything but to collect my traps together; no time to examine the implications or indeed to speculate on the reasons which my new ship might have been given for the changeover. Had I, I wondered as I stood and watched the wind-direction indicator tick round and the speed slowly mount, as I felt the wind itself blow hard and steady on the back of my neck and on the out-stretched bats, had I arrived with a notation of failure, like a slave's brand? If so, I should have to try and erase it; for I liked the feel of the ship, and would be happy to deserve well of her. There were none of the antagonisms which had made the past six months so depressing.

[188]

The loudspeaker on the island crackled and Wings said: "O.K. Bring the next one on, Bats."—and I addressed myself to the first Stringbag that was wobbling towards me a hundred yards astern.

We left the Clyde, turned south, and carried out a five-day anti-submarine sweep in the Bay which was remarkable only for the complete lack of submarines. At the end of it we put into Plymouth for a night, a novelty which, like the voyage to Malta in *Illustrious* the previous year, was a concrete illustration of how the war was going.

From there we returned to the Clyde. A few days later we were off again, in company with one of *Campania's* sister-ships, *Vindex*, escorting, so rumour said, the next convoy to Murmansk.

x

We sallied out of the Clyde in the idle autumn weather and headed into the Atlantic. One of the small consolations of being a batsman was that one did not miss—as one had often missed as a pilot, being ashore and waiting to fly aboard—the long-drawn-out, expectant moment of leave-taking; the bustle and stir of the last boat hurrying out from shore to ship with stores or signals, to be hoisted the moment it came alongside, the last link cut; the pipes that never failed to wrench a little at one's heart: "Special Sea-Duty men, fall in!" "Secure the ship for sea!" And then, the first deep shudder as the engines turn over and the screw bites and the brown water seethes up under the counter and the line of the shore begins to slide past and one knows that another voyage has begun.

Now there were matters for attention: the flight-deck mobile crane—Jumbo—to be stowed in his quarters aft of the island and lashed down; guard-rails round the lift-wells to be unrigged and stowed; equipment; bats, yellow sleeves and waistcoat, fire-extinguishers, chocks, lashings, gear of every kind, to be checked and made fast—innumerable

[189]

small jobs. Slowly, as the odour and habit of the land drop astern and the ship jolts a little on the first seaward swells, minds that have been lingering over the land, the shoreside ease, turn out towards the greying west and the islands and the seas beyond. Mingled with the slight suspense there is also an ungrateful sense of freedom and relaxation, almost of escape. The unanswered letters, the neglected duties and affections, the thousand trivial anxieties of land fade with the fading hills and the departing gulls, and are replaced by a brief elegiac mood, a distilled sweetness of regret.

What lay ahead, among the squalls that were already gathering on the horizon to the northward? In truth, nothing very harrowing. The long and savage battles of the Russian convoys, which had been real enough and reached their climax with the ill-fated P.Q. 17 of August 1942, were over. The German battleships had been eliminated one by one, and the majority of the aircraft had been withdrawn into the crumbling fortress of Germany; only the U-boats slunk persistently round the fringes of the convoy and kept our strikes of two Swordfish and a Wildcat at constant readiness. As the voyage reached its climax, in the straits between North Cape and Bear Island, it was not unusual to have seven aircraft in the air on search or strike at the same time and to do thirty or more landings, in awkward conditions of swell and low wind-speed, between midnight and midnight.

Kola Inlet, when we reached it, seemed hardly worth the trouble of a twelve-day voyage, a low, uneven fjord, its sides mottled with grey rock and scrub and stunted pine, all bathed in a nostalgic sunshine that was strong and warm on one's face. Such weather, well up within the Arctic Circle, though, paradoxically enough, farther east than Suez, was a surprise; one had expected, even at the end of the summer, a state of cold, eternal blizzard. Ashore there was nothing but a muddy track and a mass of barbed wire manned by blank, incurious but quite unequivocal sentries; Murmansk we never saw; and our only contact with the Russians was in the cordial, heated and unintelligible atmosphere of a gathering in the wardroom following the visit of a concert party from the Moscow Conservatory of Music. Any warmth of feeling so generated was somewhat dispersed by stories on board—that the British and American equipment so laboriously delivered was promptly re-stencilled "Made in Dnepropetrovsk", and that all news of the convoys and their adventures was carefully suppressed.

Each evening, as the daylight faded imperceptibly into the dusk of night, the northern sky was lit from zenith to horizon with the long, luminous curtains, rippled as if by some fitful draught blowing through inter-stellar space, of the Aurora Borealis.

The long voyage home tended to be more eventful. On the first of the two runs made by *Striker* it was the U-boats, which succeeded in torpedoing two merchantmen at the stern of the convoy just as we were frantically trying to clear the wreckage of a Stringbag whose undercarriage had collapsed on landing and which, quite arbitrarily and unexpectedly, caught fire as we were hauling the corpse up the deck; on the second occasion it was the weather which blew up into the first of the winter gales and had us rolling so wildly that it was impossible to keep one's feet on deck and made handling aircraft a tense and terrifying business.

With the days exactly and briefly measured into twelve hours of daylight and twelve of darkness, and the flight-deck already becoming bleak and inhospitable, we were resigned to a wretched winter on the same beat when we were abruptly taken off it, the squadrons were sent ashore, and the most reliable rumour had it that the ship was to do a ferry-trip to the Far East with spare aircraft for the newly-formed Pacific Fleet. And so it turned out. With real regret I learnt that they would have no immediate further need for a batsman. I was no more enamoured of the job than I had been; but the ship herself, practising that tolerant discipline by which her company were expected to work themselves to a standstill when necessary but were left, at other times, as free and unrestricted as possible, had made it bearable. Now I was out of a job, and, as events were to disclose, finished with the sea for the remainder of the war. It was left to others, including my unfortunate successor in *Campania*—who received a deserved M.B.E. for it—to work the convoys throughout the black and bitter winter, the ship ribbed with the ice of frozen spray, flying continuously through the twenty hours of darkness and the four of twilight that passed for day, and assailed by U-boats in their last, desperate attempt to regain their former ascendancy.

So perverse is the human mind that there were times when, as I sat at the trestle-table which I was pleased to call my "desk" in the secure fug of an office in the Admiralty, I found myself regretting my good fortune. Was this merely a symptom of that infirmity by which danger and discomfort appear so attractive once one is oneself safe and bored? Or was it another phase of that deeper, endless conflict, which the contingencies of war exacerbate, in which men find themselves for ever on trial at the bar of their own doubts and fears, a conflict the issue of which, no matter how much evidence is assembled for the defence, remains always unresolved?

Afterthoughts

CONCLUSION

Afterthoughts

SEA FLIGHT purports to be no more than the more
or less factual account of what happened to one Fleet
Air Arm pilot between the years 1940–45. What
happened to one happened to many, but not to all. I was
luckier than most in the aeroplanes I flew, in the actions I
was involved in, in the stations I served on, and in the
crashes I walked away from. There were many who were
less lucky. There were pilots who had no crashes, and
pilots who had only one—though it is worth remarking
that in two years in carriers I never saw a pilot killed or
injured deck-landing. There were many who fired far
more, and better-aimed, shots in anger than I ever did;
and not a few who fired even less. There were some who
were killed on their first operation, and some who were killed
on their last. War is like that, and no virtue accrues to a
man by reason of the things that happen to him. Some
people, of course, have a talent for war, and acquire merit,
quite justly, by employing it: Dickie Cork, who was killed
finally—through no fault of his own—in a trivial and
utterly unnecessary accident at Trincomalee in 1944, was
one of these. And there were others. I, as readers of this
book will have gathered, was not one of them. I did what
then appeared to be my best, and what was probably about
two-thirds of a best; for war is an encourager of bad habits,
limiting one's responsibilities, narrowing one's outlook, and
offering frequent opportunities for time-wasting.

Now, after nearly ten years, I still find it hard to equate
in my mind individual experience and total experience, the

public rhetoric and the private meiosis, the accredited hate and the actual indifference. The melancholy truth seems to be that no normally constituted person dislikes his country's enemies or is enamoured of war sufficiently to clamour for the employment of the latter against the former; nor dislikes war sufficiently to resist being pushed into it on occasion. Most of us lead uneventful enough lives, heaven knows, and the prospect of a little, not too dangerous, excitement has a subtle appeal. Such rakes' progresses follow a familiar course.

For those who have a bent for it, of course, war provides such a fufilment as no other trade can give. To those who have no such bent, it provides none; though it may indeed act as a dangerous stimulant, even to them. I cannot remember often feeling honestly and deeply bitter about it. In its more unpleasant moments one might view with romantic regret the other things that one might—but almost certainly would not—have been doing at the age of twenty-one or twenty-two; though the memory, for me, of two years at the Cambridge Law School tended to keep such fantasies within bounds. On the other hand, the impact of flying, the general mood of war, a little more reckless, a little more intense than that of normal life, and tinged with a noble and pervading melancholy, touched off in me a fuse of poetry which personal pleasures and disasters since have only set to smouldering.

Poetry, with its exact depiction of states of mind and emotion and its latent reserves of association—every word vibrating on a wave-length used by English poets since Chaucer—its compression and its special aptitude for colouring the mind of both poet and reader, poetry was the mode of speech that matched most faithfully the fitful, contrasted and occasionally molten moods of war-time flying.

Contrary to what might be supposed, it was also the simplest, as it was unquestionably the most satisfying, method of self-expression. The right word, the musical, completed line, are rarely in doubt once they have been selected and fashioned; they ring true or false, as the notes of a piano ring true or false to the tuner; and against the tuning-fork of a perception, a sensitivity, however incompletely developed, they sound with the same assurance, the same purity. Poetry, too, has a brevity and a completeness that suited the limited creative time at one's disposal: the writing of it was by far the acutest and most clearly apprehensible pleasure of those five years, the forfeiture of it one of the few lingering regrets.

For me, as for many other people, I suspect, whether they attempted to embalm them in poetry or not, the war occasioned at unpredictable intervals rare moments of exhilaration, of tranquillity, of intensified experience; moments which, if they occur at all in our humdrum peacetime lives, do so less often and with a diminished urgency. To be familiar with danger, to be often exceedingly frightened, to have to do repeatedly a job at which mind and nerves rebel: such things, which are a commonplace in wartime, are not so readily come by nowadays. We lead sedater lives, and pay for our complacence with dulled sensibilities.

This is not a plea, incidentally, for bigger, better and more frequent wars. Far from it. I deplore, as I am incapable of understanding how any man or body of men can be reduced to considering or approving, war as the concealed revolver with which to reinforce the wooden sword of diplomacy: war, at the state of perfection to which we have brought it today, is obviously too dangerous a game to play any more; and I am no hankerer after the satisfaction—if you can call it that—of a quick death in the centre of a nuclear explosion or a slow death at the edges. No one, I suppose, hankers much after that; but it will be well for us if we keep the detailed knowledge of its unequivocal horrors, as people used to keep admonitory utterances from the Bible, like a text above our beds. For we only relate what we are afraid may happen to what has happened before; our memories are nothing if not selective; and if we only think of a future war in the terms of what we now remember of the last one—despite the text—then we shall withdraw once again the only sanction that can, in the end, make war impossible—our refusal to fight.

It is the one stimulus we shall have to learn to do without. The notion of war as the supreme sport is nearly dead: it is time that the notion of it as a conceivable mode of action between human beings, whatever the provocation, was also discarded.

Yet, even if we do succeed in abolishing war, in this century or the next, some discipline, some imposition of scarcity and discontent, will certainly replace it. We are always in a state of shaky balance between aspiration and achievement, between appetite and satiety; and the fat life of peace with its increasing abundance of material goods breeds its own reaction, a longing for a life, sparser, more frugal, more dangerous. It is the best thing in the world for a man to be frightened out of his wits once or twice a year; and a welfare world will have to provide facilities for this among its more obvious and specious benefits, or risk disintegration. War, by its very agony of spirit as by its discomforts and deprivations, provides one with a point of departure, focusing desire and aspiration away from the present and towards a future, hypothetical, remote, and far more vivid than any tangible reality.

It may be that insane powers will drive or lead us into one final, obliterating conflict. Or, as seems more probable, we may be due for half a century of border-wars, of costly, inconclusive skirmishes about our changing frontiers until the coloured races, their energies unspent and their numbers still increasing, are ready to take over the worm-eaten empires of the white man. And, one is tempted to add, the very best of luck to them!

It is of no great consequence. Even in the perspective of a decade, our joys, our sufferings, our anxieties and certainties and doubts do not count for very much. We flatter ourselves when we imagine that we are faced with a completely new set of headaches; for behind the imposing façade of our mechanical progress, behind the mushroom-shaped cloud and the jet-whine, life remains for each individual as private, as simple, as tormenting, as it did two hundred or two thousand years ago. The problems with which we are faced, the needs we have to meet, the dreams with which we console ourselves, are curiously unchanging; and if it seems that psychology, for instance, has put to rest one set of fears and superstitions, others have materialised to take their place; and if we are reasonably sure that when we die we shall not migrate to a furnace-room halfway between here and Australia or to a Christian heaven somewhere in the ionosphere, for all we know to the contrary we might as well believe that still.

No one knows in advance the day by the calendar or the hour by the clock when he will die; he only knows "that death, a necessary end, will come when it will come".

It is the only end he does know. When people talk loosely of ends and means, we may justly retort: "What ends?" We are not concerned with them; they are beyond our reach. We are concerned with continuity, with the doing: all the rest is ashes.

For this reason, because war, unlike peace, has a definite end, a date on which an armistice will be arranged, and to this one's mind is bent, it is outside the true course of human affairs and sterile. The fact of its completion reduces it to the unimportance of a race or a football match; and after the cease-fire one is aware that all that has been achieved is a decision. Like so many footballers we leave the field at the end of the game and go home—to the unpaid bills and the mortgage and the vigilance of the neighbours. The miracle for which we had half-hoped had failed us, and we were faced with a different truth: the end had supplanted the means in our scale of values, and was worthless in advance.

From this fruitless exercise in human perversity, nevertheless, there were certain things worth retrieving: the moments of exhilaration, of tranquillity, of intensified experience. They were the waste-product of violence, part of no pattern, irrelevant to the purpose in hand; but they stay in one's memory after many other things, that seemed of greater weight at the time, have been rubbed out. They are the souvenirs which one brought back out of the ruins.

OTHER MEMOIRS FROM SEAFORTH PUBLISHING

Seaforth Publishing have re-released a number of classic
World War II naval memoirs, some of which are listed below.

THE BATTLE OF THE NARROW SEAS
**The History of Light Coastal Forces in the Channel
and North Sea 1939–1945**
Peter Scott

' A magnificent story. ... To read this book is to relive the excitement,
the determination and the optimism that were the defining features
of the young men of Coastal Forces in the Second World War.'
Antony Hichens

*246 x 189mm, 320 pages, 120 colour and b/w illustrations, hardback,
ISBN 978-1-84832-035-2, £25*

THE WHEEZERS & DODGERS
The Inside Story of Clandestine Weapon Development in World War II
Gerald Pawle

The fascinating story of the Admiralty's Department
of Miscellaneous Weapon Development, the so-called 'Wheezers and
Dodgers', and the many ingenious weapons
and devices it invented, improved or perfected,
told by one of a group of officers who were charged with
the task of winning the struggle for scientific mastery.

*198 x 129mm, 304 pages, 16 b/w photographs, paperback,
ISBN 978-1-84832-026-0, £9.99*

STAND BY FOR ACTION
The Memoirs of a Small Ship Commander in World War II
William Donald

This is the gripping record of varied and almost incessant action that must rank
among the most thrilling personal accounts of the war at sea. From Norway in
1940, to convoy duty on the East Coast, the landings at Anzio and then
Normandy, this is simply an unputdownable memoir.

*198 x 129mm, 208 pages, 10 b/w photographs, paperback,
ISBN 978-1-84832-016-1, £9.99*

These, and other naval memoirs, are available through
our website at **www.seaforthpublishing.com**
Or ring our order line: 01226 734555 or 734222